SI
EVER

WILLIAM ROBERTSON

4am Books

Published in 2017 by 4am Books

William Robertson has asserted his right to be identified as
the author of this Work in accordance with the Copyright,
Designs and Patents Act 1988

ISBN Paperback: 978-1-9998115-0-1
Ebook:978-1-9998115-1-8

A CIP catalogue copy of this book can be
found in the British Library.

Published with the help of Indie Authors World

IndieAuthors
World

Dedication

For my beautiful daughter, Ava-Jane.

Whatever you decide to be, the door to my house and the door to my heart will always be open to you. Thank you for being you.

Acknowledgements

Thanks to everyone in my life – good and bad – who have led me to this moment, the best times there has ever been. To my daughter, for helping me find my way in life; to my partner Karen, and the rest of my family – sister Martine, her boyfriend Gilmore, my nephew Martin, my mum and dad. To my friend, Coyle, for first putting the idea of the marathon in my mind, and to my friend, Wallace, for being there for me in my training and life changes; to lots of other friends, too. Thanks to Kim and Sinclair for helping with publishing my book, and to Christine for helping with the punctuation and structure of the book.

Nobody does it on their own. It may look that way, but everyone gets a helping hand and I've lost count of the things and people that have helped me along the way.

This book is part of my journey through life, and hopefully you can take good points and enjoy the read

Mad Matter: "Have I gone mad?"

Alice: "I'm afraid so. You're entirely bonkers. But I'll tell you a secret. All the best people are."

Alice in Wonderland

Introduction

I believe in the fairytales and dreams of life. And why not? I'm living proof of it now, and about to share with you a story of total transformation. A person who messes everything up and gets their life back together again is my favourite kind of story, and that's what I set out to do: to be my own hero, and to share this one day in the best way I could.

I don't have any talent, no athletic background, the teacher never picked me for the football team because I couldn't run, and my family genetics are all arthritis and early death. A few years ago, doctors told me I had a deranged liver, inflamed stomach, and resting heart rate back then of 86. I weighed 21 stones, and spent my life lost in pubs, nightclubs, football tops, being overweight, and eating horrible processed food every night.

But everything changed the day my little girl, Ava-Jane, was born. Although her mum and I were not together, I made a promise on that day that I would do everything I could to be a good example. Although my progress since then has not all been straightforward – and I've experienced a few false starts – I can finally say that I have succeeded in building a new life and a new me. One which I hope will make my little girl proud.

When a man has love in his heart, he can do anything. When you come from a place of love inside of yourself and the deeper intention of adding value to others, the candle never goes out. And just as that candle light doesn't diminish by being shared, neither does love, freedom, happiness, or peace.

I'm passionate about personal development, self-improvement, and becoming a self-reliant and successful person. But this book isn't aimed at a group way of thinking; it's my personal story. And while I hope it inspires you, it's up to you to do the research on your own and let your personal effort and results speak over time.

Be as healthy as you possibly can, grow, progress, share, and help those around you. Invest in yourself, invest in health and education, build winning habits, and enjoy your personal success. And let the world around you adjust accordingly.

Prologue

August 2008

My last fight was ripping the drip wires out of my arm to break free from the restraints. A gun was pointed at my face, a guard tazered me, grabbed me, and pulled me down. I was taken to a locked ward of a hospital wing on the island of Crete. I was on my way to physical, mental, and emotional hell.

My sunshine holiday had turned into a living nightmare. What had started as a fun time in the sun with my mates, had ended with me hallucinating, running about mad, ripping up money, and babbling about religion and philosophy.

Convinced I was on drugs, security officers at the holiday resort hotel called an ambulance, and my friends watched in despair as the police fought then restrained me, before taking me off to hospital.

When I woke up, it took a few minutes to take in my surroundings and figure out where I was, then I tried to run for freedom. At the side of the building there was a veranda with a big drop – that was as far as I got before handcuffs were put on and I was chained to my bed. The authorities mocked my crying in pain for my freedom.

I was placed in a padded cell, in 80-degrees heat, with doctors looking through a spy hole every 30 minutes or so; there were lots of people who didn't speak my language, and I had no clue what was going on. Was I dead?

I learned later that I had experienced a psychotic episode, which is what happens when your mind loses touch with your own reality.

This was never how I expected my life to turn out, but my character was about to be severely tested. It was time for me to endure hardship, to accept a life with no way out, to practise being patient, and to accept that there was a deeper meaning to all of this.

There were many runs at a padded wall trying to break free, and being injected with tranquillizers, before the real thinking would all happen. I guess any person restricted of liberty would act in the same way.

Imagine the worst day of your life, the death of a loved one, the end of a relationship, a broken leg... Then imagine that horror being played in your mind and hurting so much that you piss yourself in fear, with grown men tying you down, injecting you, and then laughing at you and telling you to stop crying.

Now imagine that there's no end to all of this; imagine this is your future.

What would you do?

Chapter One

In the beginning…

These days, it seems that too many people play the blame game with a dysfunctional family; too many play the poverty card in a country with more opportunities than any other.

There's no doubt, though, my early childhood was a difficult one, highlighted by sectarianism (a common problem in the West of Scotland), poverty, alcohol, and family conflict. Life was hard.

My early childhood memories are of fights with my friends, between warring families, no peace or stability, no feeling of belonging, and just frankly being scared. I wanted to feel part of something, though, to be accepted as me.

Once my dad got called into primary school because I was refusing my lunch so that I could give my lunch money to the SCIAF (Scottish Catholic International Aid Fund) charity boxes. We had been told by the teachers that we should give help to Africa, so why wasn't it right for me to give my own lunch money? They said we should give everything, and that was all I had. What was I doing wrong? I was confused.

By the age of 10, I was hitting back on the streets to defend myself. I started to battle back and became a rebel – or a toe-rag, if you prefer – yet I was always outgoing and nice to the people I wasn't fighting with. Parents had a way of disciplining children back then, and even schools taught by hitting you with a belt on the palm of your hand. So, violence seemed an acceptable way of dealing with things.

My parents lived apart, and when I became too much for my mother to cope with, she sent me to live with my dad in a bedsit in the east end of Glasgow.

I learned that making money was a good thing, because everyone always spoke about not having money, how Christmas was hard, this was hard or that was hard. I used to ferret around the old bin sheds and make a jumble sale selling the discarded items to people on the street. Who's going to say no to a kid selling a cuddly toy? Some friends and I also collected 'ginger bottles' – glass soda bottles – as there was 10p return on every bottle. We would scavenge around scaffolding and building sites to find the bottles that had been discarded by workers, then cash them in for a decent pay-out.

Another money-making scam was to plug the old-style telephone boxes by placing a bookmaker's pen into the coin return part of the box, so that people could not get their change when they'd finished their call. Once they had left, we would nip in, remove the pen, and collect the change. Easy!

We tried all sorts of dodges to make cash, even selling magazines around the doors, and washing cars at business parks in our neighbourhood. In a good spell, we could earn around £80 a week from our efforts – and it was fun. Our reward for the hard graft was pizza or McDonalds every day for dinner; the added bonus for me was that I didn't need to be fed at home.

Going out and earning money gave me a sense of identity from a young age. And although it was really just hustling, I was with my friends and we reaped the rewards with the food we wanted. It didn't bother us if other kids laughed when we walked past them with empty ginger bottles clinking in our bags. They went home to their mums' dinners while we had 16 inch pizzas washed down with big bottles of juice.

My parents were forced into hardship in tough times, and they did they best they could with the mindset they had at those times. My mum was only 16 when she got pregnant with me. She was too young to handle that and the fall-out of being a Protestant who was having a Catholic boy's child. As time passed, their lives – separately – got better, but I'm keen to show that all fruit and life stems from the root. Understand the root and you can change the fruit.

By the time I had become a teenager, I was drinking alcohol and getting involved in gang culture. Deep down, I was really just a scared kid looking for something to belong to, something to save me. I was searching for meaning at a young age when people don't normally think that way. Going to football matches, wearing a crucifix, singing rebel songs, finding role models in the pub, copying their behaviour with Stone Island jackets and watching gangster movies – it was all part of finding something to belong to.

My behaviour got me thrown out of my school and sent to Cleveden, up near Maryhill. Nobody knew me there, which was great, and I got along well with everyone and had a really great time. There was no gang violence or divide, just me and friends enjoying school, and doing normal things. It was peaceful and I loved it.

Looking back on the great parts of my childhood, they were always spending time with my dad, following Glasgow Celtic and going to cheer on the team. Celtic playing and winning was the highlight of any fan's week back then, and I'm sure it still is today. Celtic is a fantastic team with loyal supporters, and well known all around the world. They have massive rivals in the same city, who no doubt feel the same about their club.

One of my happiest memories was when my dad got us tickets to see Celtic take on FC Hamburg in the UEFA cup. Dad's friend had arranged that we could see the players after the match, so we took along an autograph book and a camera, and my dad made me wear school trousers to make sure I looked smart. I boasted to my friends at school that I was going to meet Pierre van Hooijdonk, Paulo di Canio, and all the top stars; it was going to be the greatest night of my childhood.

Celtic got beat 2-0, but we didn't care. We were going to meet the players after the match, even though it was around

9.30pm on a school night. But at the end of the game, an official came to tell us that, due to the result, the players would not be attending the after-match reception.

Tears were pouring down my face. My dad and I had taken photos during the match, but my autograph book was going to be empty. I had been hyped up to meet my heroes for the first time, and they weren't going to show up because they had got beat. I was devastated.

I was sitting crying when this old bald man came over to talk to me and my dad. Laughing and trying to cheer me up, he said he was my Uncle Jimmy and that he would show me what he had won – the European Cup, and many more medals and trophies.

I can remember just feeling at ease with him, but I had no clue who this Uncle Jimmy was. We had our photo taken with him, and Dad was thrilled. He kept telling me that it would all make sense one day.

That old baldy man was none other than Jimmy Johnstone, the man voted the greatest ever Celtic player, revered the world over by some of the top names in football. Yet he showed me what a superstar does when the camera is turned off. He taught me about what a winner is and does. He was a real gentleman and a legend.

When he died in 2006, after a long fight with Motor Neurone Disease, fans around the globe shed a tear. He touched the hearts of millions around the world with his skill and the many accolades he won, but most importantly by who he was as a person. I'll never forget our meeting.

Despite my initial disappointment, that was the start of my Celtic journey and going to the games with my dad. These matches brought great friends into my life, and I always smile when I think back to the good times. We scraped and scrimped to visit places like Germany and the Czech Republic to see the team play. These were great memories from my childhood, being with my dad and having fun. I admit there were a few underage beers, but it was mostly about singing songs and happy times; win, lose or draw, we travelled to party and to enjoy life.

It's good to look back at those times and remind myself that my early years were not all about dark places, hardship, and being with the wrong crowd. Those great occasions following Celtic will always be with me; those happy memories will never leave.

But when I left school, I went back to stay with my mum and began hanging around again with my old friends. We would go to matches, get drunk, fight, and sing anti-British songs. Really, I was just a pain in the backside to the police and, when I was stopped and found to have a keyring with a corkscrew on me, they arrested me for carrying an offensive weapon. To compound matters, a mix-up with my court papers and those of another William Robertson who was out on bail, meant I spent five weeks on remand.

The Young Offenders Unit was like a youth club. Seriously. There are a lot of scary stories about being inside, and dangerous people, but I was put in with other guys who were under the age of 21. Prison in modern Britain is more like a youth club than the desolate, frightening borstal that you read about in books. There are pool rooms, tv, work places, education, and all the things to help prisoners feel as though they are outside while being inside. They don't have to worry about bills or any other stress; everything is taken care of.

Lots of my friends were there, too. Imagine that? So, prison was no surprise, no hardship; we'd go to the gym, watch tv, then be shown how an apple was used to smoke cannabis. I was really impressed with what people could create from nothing, so I tried it inside.

Hash or cannabis is a relaxed drug in places like Amsterdam, but it makes me and a lot of other people violent. If it can help some people's health, that's great, but it makes others aggressive, agitated, and delusional. It's a mind-altering drug, and for me, losing control of reality is deadly... as I would find out later in life.

In the Young Offenders Unit, it was all about carrying on, proving yourself, finding routine, and coming to terms with life inside. The prison officers knew lots of re-offenders, and getting out of prison was usually looked on as a revolving door – the same old faces returning again and again.

Five weeks later, I was out, back to the streets, the gangs, and that culture. I started working as a labourer with my uncle and was earning £150 a week cash-in-hand, hanging around street corners at night, drinking and picking up girls. It was the normal life for me and my pals – Celtic games, trips abroad, women, alcohol, drugs, and a weekend city centre lifestyle.

But in 2004, I was sentenced to two years in prison for an unprovoked serious assault while on a night out in Glasgow. This would change the course of events of my life.

Going into prison this time was different, and I knew I had to change for me. No drink, drugs, or anything else; this was my time to work on myself and to separate from others. There were a few fights inside, as that's what happens in prison when you choose to be different. All I wanted was peace to do my own thing, to read, educate myself, stay healthy, and focus on building the best lifestyle I could for my release.

It might sound strange, but there were parts of prison life which I actually enjoyed – when I escaped into my own mind, reading books, writing, doing press-ups and sit-ups. I would look out of the cell towards the Campsie Fells – the hills that I had visited as a boy – and imagined freedom, with waterfalls and hills. I lost eight stones in weight, became fit, and had never felt better in my life. What other prisoners saw as torture with no TV or hot food, I saw as empowerment and self-discipline. A fresh start.

But we are who we hang around with in this life, and on my release I went to the pub to celebrate, and got around the same group all over again. We just did the same things, and I have no idea how I survived the fights and assaults.

Underneath all that hard man image was someone crying out for love. I became involved in a long-term relationship, but was still trying to hold down a lifestyle of drinking, partying, and hanging out with my mates. By that stage, I had a job as a salesman and was doing well, had a beautiful girlfriend and money coming in, but I was miserable. I'd put on weight again, was struggling with gambling addiction, and my weekends focused on alcohol and drugs, or just buying things to fill my life's emptiness. I had totally lost my self-discipline.

One night I met an old friend in Glasgow and, after a few beers, we had the idea of going down to Newcastle. For some reason, we got off the train at Dumfries and got into a fight. I was charged with three serious assaults and two assaults in the one night, and sentenced to four years in prison with a third of that term off for pleading guilty.

A few months into the prison sentence, I had lost the weight and was feeling good again. I followed the same rituals, and made my peace. Maybe this was my home for life, inside my mind. Was I better off in prison, because outside didn't seem like much to go out to?

I got fitter and stronger while in prison. I won the 2000m rowing championship inside, passed exams, completed sports leader courses, and planned on making a new start when my sentence was over. On my release, I intended to leave everything behind and start again.

But I was in love, and chasing the same girl brought me to the same old mates, lots of drugs and alcohol; back to the same messy life.

I planned an escape to Greece on holiday with old friends, to blow it all. I had made up my mind that I didn't want to come back home, as I had nobody and nothing to come back to, my meaning was gone again, and I was wondering around lost. I took out bank loans, got into debt, and bought everything I needed.

My plan was to never return from Greece. I was going to have a nice holiday and give my friends the best time of their lives, with me being the life and soul of the party, then it was all going to be over. I hadn't really thought through what I was going to do after that, but I just knew I wasn't coming back with them.

I certainly didn't expect to be put into a high security mental asylum after ripping up money and being loud and out of control. But they do say that not getting what you want can be a wonderful stroke of luck!

Chapter 2

It was supposed to be a two-week holiday in Greece to celebrate time with friends, to have fun and to party. But I had made up my mind before I left Scotland that it might be the last time I would see the country again. In my mind, I had nothing and nobody to go back to, so this was going to be my final blow-out.

The holiday proved to be one big party, and it was fun for everyone around me; they loved the loud noise, alcohol and fun, the partying and loud music. I played up to that environment, but I was hurting badly whenever I had the chance to think without the loud noise and partying.

On the outside, everything looked perfect, but the loud laughing and comedy with the lads was just to hide my inner hurt of sadness. At the end of every bottle of beer and every night with another young woman, I still felt unfulfilled. I knew I wasn't living life to my potential.

What was the point in getting out of prison to only do this with my life? What was the point? Inside, I knew this wasn't for me, but over and over again I tried to cover it.

I began hallucinating, and my friends saw the change in me overnight. I began running about mad, ripping up money, and talking about religion and philosophy. Thinking I was high on drugs, the security staff at our holiday hotel called an ambulance, and I was taken off to hospital.

When I got there, I ripped the medical tubes out of my arms and had a gun pointed at me. I was beyond understanding at that stage, so told them just to shoot me. They tazered me and transferred me to a mental asylum. I pissed myself in fear; I was faced with a life of no way out, not even a change of clothes.

It's difficult to describe just how awful the Greek asylum was, but imagine a sauna with a padded cell around it. The meals were mainly half-chewed chicken, which someone else had obviously eaten before me, and every few hours, groups of security men would come in, pin me down, strap me to my bed, then inject me with drugs to keep me sedated. The only time I felt any peace was when I would clasp my hands, lay back, and look inwards to myself.

My family were worried sick and fighting to get me back home. People in the local community helped my dad out by gathering money to pay for his flights to come and see me. Eventually, with the help of the British Embassy, I was flown back – heavily sedated – to Glasgow.

For a while, I'd thought my life was over, stuck in Greece, with no way out. Now I was coming home, still broken, but the fresh rain in Scotland felt so beautiful on my face as I came off that plane. Maybe, in order to gain anything, we must first lose everything.

From the airport, I was taken to Stobhill Hospital to be assessed, but I ran away at the first opportunity. My parents took me back, and this time police officers stood beside nurses as I was restrained, then sedated, and placed in the high security wing.

It was just me and hospital, but it wasn't so bad. At least I could understand the language, I wasn't sunburnt, and I knew that in this country I could outlast the pain. I'd had years of experience in solitary confinement, overcoming it all with endurance and outlasting anything or anyone who thought they could break me.

The reality is, as with any fight in life, the whole time you are only ever fighting yourself. I was big on Gandhi back then, and passive resistance; when there is no way out, you go internally and create a phenomenal force that nothing or nobody can get to. Your self-discipline sets you free, as it's something inside that nobody else can reach.

The years between 2008 and 2010 were long and tough for me, and spent mostly alone. I was coming to terms with being labelled with an illness labelled schizoaffective disorder, which is a combination of both schizophrenia and bipolar. No half measures then!

Glasgow has a great personality as a city, but deep down I believe that's because it's a city which knows adversity; a city with heroes and courage, but the over-laughter mostly comes from a lot of healed pain.

After I was discharged from hospital, I went back to my old lifestyle with crowded pubs, clubs, and football. Before long, I was off on holiday again, doing the same things – drinking, singing, and meeting women.

On one night out in Magaluf, a friend and I were accused by police of being drug dealers. I'll be honest, I have taken drugs but I have never sold them; it's a business I never involved myself in, and is probably a big reason why I'm still alive today. The Spanish police hit us and put us in the back of their van, then took us to our hotel. They ripped the room apart and took about 1000 euro from us, told us we weren't being charged but would be fined 50 euro each. We were left stunned, broke, and with black eyes and broken ribs.

After each crazy holiday, I returned to Glasgow and back to the old routine. But privately, my life was becoming darker and lonelier, and laughter no longer seemed to be enough any more.

This was the beginning of me looking for deeper answers to the life around me.

Glasgow is a city I will always love. I love the people, too, but the alcohol and drug culture is big for the masses, and the crowds all do the same things and follow the same people into the same environments.

I began to go my own way, to take charge and try to find a lifestyle I could enjoy. I started writing, trying new educational courses, meeting new people. But my old friends and family couldn't understand why I didn't want to do anything with them any more, and after a few weeks I was tempted back, spending time with old mates, getting drunk, questioning my life and relationships. I weighed 21 stones (around 55kg) and my life was going nowhere.

The final straw was the day I followed a huge Orange Walk (Protestant march), wearing a Celtic top and carrying a piece of paper explaining the law and why I was joining in. Religion has been an issue in Glasgow for many years, and too many people have lost their lives to the violence and hatred that is linked to it. I wanted to walk in among the marchers to make a stand, but I was stopped by the police and told to stay away.

When I kept rejoining the march, I was arrested for my own safety but wasn't charged. I realised then that people singing war songs and promoting hatred on both sides was really just about people following a crowd. It became clear that Glasgow was just not ready for peace.

But maybe it wasn't Glasgow that had to change; maybe it was me.

Chapter 3

Travelling around Scotland brought me peace with every step. When I had been locked up in Greece, and at other times in prison, I had always imagined myself finding freedom and peace. And now I had.

I had given up everything and everybody, taken up meditation, and headed off to the mountains and countryside of Scotland with no hope, no parents, no help, no money, no nothing. Just me and an iPhone.

If heaven is a place, then it can be no more beautiful than the Scottish hillside, lochs and mountains, that's for sure. On my travels I would sit in stillness, look at the sky and enjoy some food. I've always been outgoing, so meeting new people on my travels was easy and everyone was nice to me. Strangers helped me to regain my faith in humanity again, simply by giving me their time, telling me stories, advising on places to visit, relating stories of their own journey, having normal everyday conversations that I'd never experienced. Growing up, all I knew was the news, football, politics, and who had been drunk at the weekend.

Maybe everything I had been searching for had been on my doorstep all this time. The waterfalls at the Campsie Fells, Loch Lomond, the Cairngorm mountains, the Samye Ling Buddhist Centre near Lockerbie — these were all treasures to enjoy.

Finding that peace led me to a new relationship over the internet, one which grew quickly. We met and became parents fast. I was going to be a dad; this was everything, wasn't it? Family, and a chance to correct everything?

We went on holiday to Africa together, which proved to be a life-changing experience for me. After a safari trip, we were offered food from animals in the zoo. I refused, and made a promise that day never to eat animals ever again.

Sadly, our relationship didn't work out, though we tried several times. This time, rather than head for the pub again, I went back to the hills and mountains, travelling around Scotland, finding peace.

Although we were no longer together, when I heard that my ex-partner was in labour, a friend of my mum's ran me to the hospital. At 18:29 on the 30th January, 2013, our daughter Ava-Jane was brought into the world.

I could not stop crying. I looked into my baby girl's eyes and promised I would do everything that I possibly could to make her happy, and to be a role model in her life. And when you make promises in life, you must fulfil them.

I was determined to turn my life around for her. So, I went back to my blueprint for peace – meditation, hills and lochs, watching the monk called Ajhan Brahm on YouTube, feeding and programming my own mind with education and insights from outside my old social surroundings.

I bumped into Coyle, an old friend I'd known at primary school. When we were young, he used to go out running while the rest of us were drinking and chasing girls. He told me that he now ran half-marathons, which sparked my interest.

But, as usual, I wanted to take things a step further. When he said he was entering a half-marathon at Blackpool, I suggested we do the full marathon. Coyle stuck to the half marathon, as his pace was fast and he liked to run to better his time, but I signed up for the full race.

At that time, I hadn't a clue about running, and didn't even know how long a marathon was (26.2 miles, as I later discovered!). I just like to learn as I experience things.

In the local gym, I used the sauna and steam room to relax my mind rather than to work out. There, I met so many amazing people from all walks of life. I found it easier to talk to these strangers about the marathon than to my old friends, who wouldn't have understood. There was one man in his seventies who I particularly enjoyed listening to; old Pat had run marathons himself, and he gave me plenty of encouragement and advice. Always smiling and happy, he enjoyed life.

Pat admitted that when he had taken up running in his younger days, it had been a lonely pastime as all his mates were in the pub. But he said that the lonely road would make sense in the long run, and shared with me his mantra for the journey: Smile every mile!

Sadly, Pat died just before I ran my first marathon, but he is still in inspiration to me and I will always be grateful for his advice and encouragement.

On the 7th of April, 2013, I turned up at the starting line in Blackpool, wearing a jogging suit, hillwalking shoes – and no game plan. Many athletes take part in marathons as a test of endurance, to compete with others in the elite of distance running, but many more entrants are charity runners, fun runners, and ordinary people keen to dig deep and try this for themselves.

I had no charity sheets, no sponsors, no training, no plan for running, and no proper clothes, either. I had lost two stones in weight since becoming vegetarian after the Africa trip, but I still weighed a hefty 19 stones.

That 26.2 miles was finished step by step and inch by inch in 4 hours 53 minutes. By the end, I was blistered, bruised, and chafing all over; my physical body was in bits, but mentally I felt totally fulfilled.

I hadn't been running for significance, or to prove a point to others. I was running to take charge of my life and my health, and to show my daughter how I'd changed my life. Everything in life means more when you do something for someone other than yourself.

I didn't want my life to be judged on my past, but on my present and my future. I wrote in my personal journal: *When you go through tough times in life, it's time to act in a way you would love your kid to act in the same situation.* This thought inspired me, and still does.

After the marathon, Coyle had a pint; it was celebration time. This time, I stuck to fresh orange juice and tap water. I'd used alcohol for many reasons in my life, but now I just did not need it. I felt good. I felt happy. And I knew this was just the beginning; I could do better.

When I got home, I bought running shoes, started to train around the park, and signed up for another marathon — in Dundee this time.

My ex-partner and my daughter came along to see me run, and this spurred me on to do better. This time I looked more professional with shorts and running shoes, but it turned out to be one of the hottest days of the year – 25 degrees – with weather warnings!

I wore a cotton t-shirt and discovered that blood-stained nipples is just another part of the learning curve of running marathons. However, I finished in 4:29, almost half an hour faster than my time in Blackpool.

Running had become a huge part of my life, and I signed up for the Loch Ness marathon next. This time, I ran for charity, to try and add value to other people's lives. Funnily enough, I always felt guilty asking people for sponsorship and donations, as I had never liked asking anybody for anything. Maybe that's why I never got much in the past. My dad always used to say to me, 'If you don't ask, you don't get.'

None of my friends or family ran. Coyle was the only runner I knew, but he had cut back on his training and wasn't doing many events any more, so this time I was on my own. But everywhere I went people always gave me their time and best self. On the bus journey north, I got chatting to a lovely girl – a singer – and she even gave me a book to read when we reached our destination.

I had started to keep a social media blog of my journey through life, talking about the beautiful Scottish scenery and using meditation. And, despite my bad grammar and spelling, I found a growing number of people were beginning to take an interest and to give me support.

I finished the Loch Ness marathon with bleeding nipples again — but with a marvellous time of 3:44. To my delight, my aunt and uncle were waiting at the finishing line and recorded a video of me finishing – something to show my daughter in future years.

Their support that day was a huge bonus. They were probably one of the few couples I knew who had stayed married, and had always helped and looked after me when I was young.

I returned to Glasgow with a different mindset, a different level of understanding, and a different level of health. My passion and lifestyle had changed, but people look at you differently when you progress in life.

I could dramatize things and talk about crime, prison, tell you about women, drugs, and a party life like they do in Hollywood films, but my advice is to stay away from anyone who talks like this or anyone who tells you that people make money through crime. Make your life and lifestyle an example, not a warning. There's so much more to life than the bottle; it's ruined more friendships and families than you could ever imagine.

I hope my story will provide you with a straightforward approach to my blueprint now – the pattern, lifestyle, and the winner's mindset which I've found after years of failure. I have learned through plenty of trials and errors, in finding new role models, reading amazing books, and sticking with my 'why'.

Who are your role models? Who is inspiring you? Who is an example? Who is a warning? They are all relevant in how you create the best you. I will never lose my way, because I will never lose my 'why'. So, what's your 'why'? Why do you wake up in the morning? Why do you share what you do with others?

When you've finished reading my story, I just want you to remember the name of a person who overcame the odds, then you can use that person in your own story one day. Or hand this book on to someone else. My life change was not inspired by people *around* me; it was everything *inside* me — the books, the kind strangers, the process, and my 'why'.

I'm not saying that nights out, travel, women, and football matches, are not good or fun, but they are only something people use to fill themselves up for whatever reason. I come from a background of drama, of council estate politics, of people keeping up with the Joneses and looking rich but never being rich.

There are plenty of people who will tell you that you can't do something, or not to read books, or be healthy or be more of yourself. Just walk away from them. Be all you can be, and stay away from those who try to stop you living your dream; only listen to people with proven results.

There's a lot of temptation out there. Lots of people who will say 'try this', 'do that', 'why do you not drink alcohol?' They'll laugh and tell you that no great story started with a salad, and so on, but that only tells you what sort of programmes they watch and what books they read.

Every time I met someone from my past, they asked the same thing: 'What do you do for money?' They didn't want to know about my college work, the training, the home education I had done. All they saw was me running and training, and tried to put a price on me. In modern day Britain, public libraries, museums, parks, and nature all cost nothing (you can make a donation if you want), but so many people only pay attention to what they pay for. So, they miss out on the things that matter.

I couldn't afford *not* to walk in the park. I couldn't afford *not* to read books. While these people were on their phones calling, texting, and sending 'selfies' as part of their city life, I used my iPhone to turn the video on myself and add value to others.

I believe I have a message of value to share, and I'm willing to be unpopular to deliver that message. You can look for me on YouTube – search William Robertson.

Chapter 4

I have had people questioning me the whole journey; people trying to talk me out of my vision and my dream, even people who loved me telling me to relax and that I didn't need to change. But they just couldn't see what I could, and I had a promise to fulfil to my daughter.

The culture in Glasgow, where I was raised, is a culture where it's okay to lose, it's okay to settle and go to the pub. With our national football team and in other sports, we always suffer last minute losses, hard luck stories, then drown our sorrows as a nation.

So, what I had chosen was something completely different to the way in which I had been raised. I felt it was time to play the game and take charge of my own results in life, enjoy my own life, build a new lifestyle, and give my everything to what I'm passionate about, for who and what I love.

It was the end of 2013 now, and instead of celebrating the New Year with friends or family, I woke up at 4am and ran 26.2 miles on my own around the city. I decided that in 2014 I would run 2014 miles for Yorkhill Hospital Sick Kids' charity, and wrote in my notes that I would attempt to inspire people along the way.

The 'resolutions' I set were that I would stick to turning the iPhone on myself to make videos of the journey; write blogs; run to and from college; read all the books and watch all the seminars I could; try to encourage other people in this forward-moving journey; and make myself better every day.

My running friend, Coyle, introduced me to his mate, Wallace, who became a good friend of mine. We booked to take part in the Amsterdam marathon after we had enjoyed a trip up north to Nairn, running on Scottish beaches which I had previously visited alone. Wallace knew why I ran, he knew the kind of people and trouble I had once been involved with, but he's a smart guy. He's never been in bother in his life, and has many friends; basically, he is just a really nice person.

All the new friends that I was meeting and travelling with shared the same characteristics; I'm even friends with police officers now! But it's not about the title or the job which people have; it's about their character and why they do what they do as people that's important. People who focus too much on a title usually have nothing else to talk about.

The more miles I ran, the better I felt, and I knew I was living the life that I had created. I also found that people came into my life through this new way of living, by me being open and using my lifestyle as an example.

One day I was running alone on the West Highland Way near Drymen. I had recently watched a documentary of how calves have their milk taken from them to benefit humans, and are put to death for meat called veal. Looking into the cows' eyes that day as I passed their field, I felt as though I could see into their inner being and world. And that was the day that I decided to become vegan.

Those cows had their calves taken away from them; I didn't have my daughter with me, so I felt we shared something. I was going to move forward and make vital changes in my life for me, for my daughter, and for the animals.

Glasgow is not a place where men become vegan because of animals; it's a rough city, but I believe that the love I have for the animals can drive away any criticism in the long run.

I had become vegetarian before I went vegan, so my initial weight loss was through changing to vegetarian. I lost even more when I became vegan.

I am not going to question how other people eat, or what other people do. I am only living by my own example, my own peace, my own choices, and what I believe is right through my own life experiences. It is a lifestyle which I have chosen and created.

My aim was to keep on becoming the best version of myself every day, and at the same time trying to add value to others. That was the plan; that simple.

When I had become vegetarian, I saw my weight drop from 21 stones to 19 stones. After running a few marathons, lots of miles and lots of fun, I lost more weight until I reached around 15 stones.

When I decided to become vegan, I was initially eating the junk food which many vegans eat, like the cakes and substitutes to meat. But one day I went into my local fruit and vegetable shop in Glasgow, and said: 'I am vegan but don't have a clue about vegetables, or how to eat healthily, can you help me?' The staff laughed at first, but then one guy handed me a free book on how to cook vegetables, and that was the start of another new life experience: total health!

My weight dropped again, and my mental peace and progress started to excel at a new level. I was recovering faster from runs, needing less sleep, and wanting to study and learn more. But it was time to put the new food choices to work at a marathon.

I ran the Manchester Marathon in 3:11, which was a big drop on the 3:44 at Loch Ness and a massive improvement from my Blackpool marathon the previous year. I'd now reached the one year anniversary of running, and was finishing two hours faster – brilliant! I know it looks simple, and lots of people see me smile all the way round the course, but the smile comes from a psychological belief of knowing my why; the smile represents my past, and my heart represents my future.

I don't see running as hard work any more, but more as a lifestyle and a movement. I also view it as an expensive experience, because what would be the price of not running? What would be the price of not putting my own health first?

After sharing my journey on my blog, and running my target of 2014 miles in 2014 long before that summer, I discovered on a twitter news feed that people ran ultras (which is anything beyond normal, and normal is 26.2 miles). Some ran 30, 50, even 70 miles. But the one that struck me most covered 100 miles. 100 miles in the one race! That's almost the distance from my house to England. I needed to try it.

So, I went on Facebook pages and groups, asking for tips and advice on how to do the 100 miler; I was full of enthusiasm, even though I had only been running for 12 months. Nobody gave me the go-ahead; everyone said wait, don't throw yourself in, get a training plan, a coach. But when I looked closer at the people who were responding, it was really people who had never run 100 miles themselves, yet they were offering me this advice.

With a marathon, most runners have a training plan and tip book to follow, but at ultra-marathons you become your own boss because you have to know what works for *you* over 100 miles. With endurance sports, you have to be your own health expert, nutritionist, doctor, and everything else along the way.

So, I thought I'd give it a try, and think about it later. First, I ran the 35 mile Ultra at Kintyre in beautiful Scottish scenery, and thoroughly enjoyed the whole experience.

I had been reading blogs on the 100 miles, and I decided to take the full ultra kit for 100 miles – including food and everything needed to run a long distance – but it really wasn't needed for only a 35 mile race. It proved to be a real rookie error to run such a short ultra with a large backpack.

The Kintyre race was on the second Saturday in May, and two days later I also ran the Belfast Marathon at the last minute with a friend. He was keen to beat his PB of 3:44, so we headed over, ran around the course, and finished in 3:21. It was brilliant, and his family were at the finish to support us, which was nice.

Ultra races are very different from ordinary marathons; no crowds, no support, it's just you. But that is when I thrive, as it's more of a psychological battle over distance. When there are crowds, I can draw energy from people cheering, waving, and being there. I had always enjoyed being the centre of attention in my old life, so the marathon was like another party.

With ultras, however, the attention is on the inner part of yourself; the deeper part. And I love it! It's like a boxing match with yourself, so it's right up my street.

When it comes to positive psychology (or what I term post-traumatic growth), then my example speaks more than any words ever could. When the chips are down, when there is no energy left and no money in the bank, that's when the best version of me shows up to fight back. I captain my own ship in this life, so to take on a 35-mile event like this was brilliant and I rose to the challenge again.

My life was starting to improve. I was passing college courses, training for a 100 miler, and finding myself in the public eye for health and running. Looking back, finding that platform to touch and inspire other people's lives would never have happened without many of my earlier struggles, but having the opportunity to help others by my example made it all the more meaningful. Now I was ready to run the 100 miles, and my mum, dad, sister, her boyfriend, Gilmour, and my young nephew would come down for the event.

Through all the knockdowns, the hurt, the loss, and the pain led me to a more authentic and real version of myself, and anytime I had the chance to see my daughter, I felt so grateful and happy. Without her, I would not be the man I am today. So I thank her every day in meditation.

The changes in my life and thoughts led me to finally make peace with my own parents, to forget the past, and to thank them for all they did in bringing me into this world to be a self-reliant and successful man. Everyone can say people should do this or that with their life. But rebuilding a relationship with your parents is something I would recommend to anyone, in order to fully develop into a responsible adult who moves forward in their own initiative.

Not getting what you want in life can sometimes be the most valuable thing that can happen to you. It makes you open up further, look into more meaning, and have richer and stronger relationships. But most of all, it makes you forgive. And if you can do that and let go, you can live a life bigger than you could ever have imagined; one of deep peace, fulfilment, and joy.

Everyone wants to be pleased, so most will choose quick-fix pleasures like coffee, alcohol, or even drugs to shift that emotion. Yet deep down, what we are all searching for is not a quick fix, but lasting love and fulfilment. No-one should ever feel they are not strong, powerful, and have meaning in life, because everyone has greatness in them. Every human being has the power to help, to change, to transform, and to simply be there for another life.

What you have to remember is that there is simply no progress in life without struggle. So, whatever you go through, you must deal with it, accept it, and push past the pain to realise your own greatness. You need to believe in yourself. The pain is simply leading you to awaken the giant within yourself, so don't ever cover that up!

In my case, I took to the 100-mile challenge as a vegan marathon runner aiming to be an ultra-running athlete, and with a vision that this would help me to reach new heights.

Chapter 5

Why tackle a 100-mile ultra marathon so soon? Every-one said I should do smaller ultras and work up to the 100, but my view was that I would rather try the 100 and fail than just think about it my full life.

Nowadays, I don't listen to people much when they try to discourage me with the things I want to do in life. I don't put limits on myself, and I would never discourage anyone else. When I was at school, my teacher said I couldn't run so he never let me in the football team. As a result, I gave up on sports at a young age; looking more deeply, I really gave up on myself because of what others said to me. I thank that teacher now as he, along with lots of others throughout my life, have taught me that other people's opinions do not have to be my reality. Instead, I listen to my own inner voice and how I feel.

So, I went ahead and signed up to the 100-ultra marathon taking place in Peterborough, England, because I wanted to test myself as a human being. And I'm happy that I did.

What should have been a five-hour drive turned out to be a 12-hour bus journey. As I was heading down, I got a phone call from the woman at the bed and breakfast where I had booked to stay. Apparently, there had been a flood and I would need to find somewhere else to stay. I told her not to worry about it, as these things happen. I was just so focused on ultra marathon that no small thing could redirect my thinking.

I received a text from the B&B lady later, thanking me for my attitude and being so understanding, and she paid for a room at a hotel for me. I was really grateful for that, as it was a bit more expensive than what I had originally paid for the night at the B&B.

When I arrived in Peterborough, it was time for me to look into a plan for the 100 miles, rather than just to run like I have in the past. I didn't really know where to start, but I do now! My family had offered to help by getting the proper food for me to take during the race, but they ended up with a lot of the wrong things, like crisps and cookies, because they don't understand much about being a vegan.

During a 100-miler, food is very important, and it's one of the areas where I went wrong. I probably only packed what I would normally eat on an average day but with a few energy gels included. 1 had a packet of potatoes, beans, five energy gels, and one or two trek bars (a vegan favourite) out of the 15 I brought. Bananas, which were handed out at the aid station, proved to be a blessing, and the rest was just Irn-Bru.

I had asked my mum to bring Weetabix and soya milk for me to eat at one of my stops, but there was only almond milk and it went all lumpy, which made me feel sick. I managed to swallow two spoonfuls but it was horrible, and I to press on and think about food again in 10 miles. This did hurt later on in the race when I was starving, but it was my own fault.

My nephew ran alongside me while I ate, and that gave me a big lift, while my sister made a banner saying 'Smile every mile', and I wanted to do well as it was the first time they had all been at an ultra-race event. It was great to have my family there, although sometimes too many people can be distracting when you only take five or ten minutes to stop and eat. But I gave them all a cuddle and thanked them for being there as I made my way round the course.

My sister was a great help. She stayed up all night, sorted the food at my tent, made sure I was eating a bit, and tried her very best to help me without even knowing what to do.

I was dehydrated and starving a lot during the closing stages of the race, as it was a hot day, but I never judge a day by the weather; I judge it on the effort I give, and I know I gave my best.

My plan for the 100 was to run every 25 miles in under 5 hours. (In my head, I was calculating four marathons back-to-back at sub 5.) The first 20 miles I was at 3:18, then by 70 miles I was at 14:57, so all I had left was 30 miles – and I felt great. If I had been racing the 40 miles, I would have finished in 6th place; if I was racing the 70 miles, I would have finished in 4th place. But I was racing the 100, so none of that mattered!

As I reached the last 30 miles, running into the dark, I was sitting great and feeling good. I had bought a head-lamp from Amazon but had never tried it before, so I put it on but couldn't see a thing, and the back-up headlamp was just as bad. About three miles into the 8th lap of the 10 miles up the hill and into the trees, I couldn't see, which meant I couldn't go fast. Instead, I had to just pick my way slowly and carefully along.

I told myself this was the real character-building part, but then I kicked a boulder and went over on my ankle and hurt my knee. As I got to my feet, I felt sick and wondered if I'd broken my ankle. But I hobbled on.

By the time I got to 80 miles, I was dehydrated, starving, and in a lot of pain. I had gone without water for nearly two hours. My sister was trying to help so she filled bottles up, but you have to unscrew the bottles to get water – it's too tough trying to drink from the tip – and I dropped the bottles a few times. This wasn't good.

Looking back, the first 70 miles of that race was a pleas-ure and I had raced well. Yet, what might surprise you, it's the last 30-mile stretch which was my favourite. I learned so much about myself and what I could pull through. I was crying in pain as I moved forward slowly, but I was deter-mined to complete the 100 miles. Time was irrelevant now; all I was focused on was the finish.

Just 15 months before that race, I weighed almost 21 stones and was in poor health, yet here I was, almost at the end of my first 100-mile ultra marathon at the age of 28. My life had changed so much. I'm a very independent person now, but it meant so much to have my family with me and so much support from other people.

As I hobbled along, I thought of the support of my family, the friends I had made through running, and how grateful I was for their encouragement. Tears were rolling down my face, and I don't know yet whether I couldn't see much in front of me because of the headlamp or the tears. But I could see the stars, and I felt really happy – despite the pain – knowing I was alive and living this life.

It might sound crazy, but it opens up a deep connection to my inner self for me when I push the boundaries then push past them, saying 'I'm strong', and never giving up. Running 100 miles was a big step up from anything I had tackled before, but what an experience! I kept saying over to myself, 'When things go wrong, you push forward, big man. You adapt and you overcome. This is yours, even if you have to crawl. You came here to finish and that's what you're doing.'

And I did!

To sum it all up, I finished the entire race in 24:43. I completed the first 70 miles in under 15 hours, and hobbled the last 30 to the finish. When I eventually got there, I was trying to say thanks to people who were clapping, but I was holding back the tears. I was emotional, but I even astonished myself that I had managed to keep going.

My dad treated me to a night at Blackpool, so that we could break up the journey back to Glasgow a bit. But when I got in his car, I started crying and felt dizzy. By this time, it was two o'clock in the afternoon and I realised I hadn't eaten anything since about 5am.

I was totally dehydrated, and when I tried to get out of the car at a motorway service station, I collapsed on the ground, crying. I had never felt like that before, and I was scared. But I drank some fruit juice and ate raw fruits, and felt a lot better.

I learned so much during the 100, about the correct food, the importance of water, and having proper equipment. I met a few great and inspirational people on the journey, too. I ran the first 15 miles or so with Vic, a girl I had met through running, and another friend, Nikki, who finished her 40 miler, too. It was good to see them both, along with Alistair, who finished his first ultra, and a guy Jerry that I met about 50 miles in. We had a great chat about life and ultras.

But the best part was when I was on my own and struggling. At one point, I took a few minutes to look at my phone at the aid station, and the support and encouragement from others on social media just made me cry again.

I can honestly say that the 100 miles changed me as a person. Lots of people will define ultra-marathons in all different ways and all different distances, but for me, it's more than a distance; it's a lifestyle. It's about continuing to run when it doesn't make sense to keep on running, in order to feel that deep emotional part of yourself that can withstand anything; to experience the feelings of freedom and independence of your full life journey; and to stand tall in the moment, being all you can possibly be.

Running long distances makes normal things seem so small in life. If the bus is late, then get the next one, or run; if someone doesn't turn up on time or if I lose something, there's no point getting worked up over it. My needs and desires in life are now a lot more simple. To run, read, write, meditate, enjoy a good night's sleep, and be around lovely people – that means the world to me. Peace, after all the craziness of my early life, is heaven.

People run ultra-marathon events for lots of different reasons. Some will continually push themselves in multi-day and country-crossing events, but I've learned through many miles and my own inner experience not to see the sport as a competition or having to prove to the world I can do things. For me, it's a lifestyle to transcend the mind and body into this emotional and spiritual state of being.

I love the fluent feelings of freedom and independence that come with being outside with nature for so long; having that peace as a survivor, as a man in charge of his own health and freedom, putting one foot in front of the other no matter what limitations the world tries to throw my way.

I can run 100 miles, but I get the same feeling now after a 10-mile run or just even talking about the journey that took me to run in the first place. I've made my peace with life, sport, and the choices that led me to where I am now.

Chapter 6

So, what do you do after running 100 miles? What's next? Another big challenge? A new life of constant adventure? Some people will climb mountains, go world travelling, and do other amazing things they do with their life and inspire so many others along the way. My journey is more internal. It's not about writing records of world travel and extreme events, it's more about having a deep peace, of joy, contentment and wellbeing that's come from a life journey into the depths of myself and to the darkest corners of my mind – to find this peace, to create this lifestyle, and to share with others. And it feels beautiful.

Nobody has it all good, but it's really about what you decide in your mind that you want to make your life about. All those miles of running have led me home to where I belong. It was about my own inner peace; my own transformation to a journey into the inner depths of my own mind. And at first it hurt; it hurt a lot. I was angry, I was bitter, and I had so much deep sorrow and a lot of tears to come out of me. But then I found peace and a love of myself that I never knew existed.

All that I had been through in life now meant I could share with others a way out, the early warning signs, an example of how to build themselves up, to train and create a lifestyle so they would never have to feel like there is no hope – the way I once did. Because if I can do it, then we can all do it.

Through deep meditation, love, ultra-running, and acceptance of myself, it led me to the journey inwards, to understand that the actions we all have as humans are our only true possessions in this life. Our actions are everything, and what matters most – our happiness, health, and freedom – are all on our own shoulders. It wasn't the mountains or challenges on the outside that changed me, it was my inner world shift that changed the outer world results I was getting. There is no failure, only results.

To explain the inner work on yourself more easily, you wouldn't expect someone who butchers animals or a drug dealer to meditate to find peace inwards. The paths that they have chosen in life are to do things with outward value, even if animals and people are hurt in the process. My journey was to find peace within myself and to use my life, mind, body, spirit, and my own transformation to develop a lifestyle of joy and contentment that I could share with my daughter, and with others in this world around me.

I know where I came from, I know my whole journey, so I am not one for preaching what's right or wrong with the world today by pointing fingers. Inner peace is a state of mind that anyone can achieve with the right intention.

If my only object in this life was about the outside world then I would never have changed, progressed, become healthy, run 100 miles, become who I am today, meditated, or even be writing this book. These all come from the inner world and from inside me.

I was inspired by a story of the Japanese Buddhist monks who used running as a way to find their inner peace. With Buddhism, there are no rules to follow or an end result of heaven or hell to look to; there is no outside source or anyone else to help you. Your own mind and your own life are your own choice, and the actions you have are your true possessions in this lifetime. It's more a philosophy than a religion and that's why I studied it, meditated, and enjoyed the great teachings from it. But I'm not a monk or a Buddha. I just liked that the guy Buddha was not born enlightened, but went on a journey like me and enjoyed the meaning.

I wake up at 4am every day to meditate first thing, in order to have time for me. I choose to put the alarm clock on for myself, to wake up for me first, to develop my mind and be all that I can possibly be. And then I give all I can in the day ahead, and try to be my best for others around me.

I love how I am living now, eating the fruits and vegetables, meditating, sleeping well, keeping hydrated, reading and educating myself, along with running outside with nature. These may be selfish things on their own, but they make me better for everyone around me. In openly sharing my lifestyle, I want to show others self-reliance, self-discipline, and self-awareness. If I can do it, as I said before, then everyone can. We can all take care of our health, get better, and add value to the life around us.

I've never felt more content, confident, and satisfied with my life, and it is such a massive change from how I used to live.

Life will throw us all tremendous blows, but if you overcome them then you will have a good life. To read is a great thing, but to read the right book at the right time makes things more special, and this book is designed to be at the right time for you.

I chose to use all the shit I had in my life as a fertiliser, just as my first teacher Ajhan Brahm (I listened to his talks on YouTube) explains: 'Only a silly gardener would throw away shit; the good gardener uses the shit as fertiliser to grow beautiful plants in the garden.'

Once I heard that, I knew that I could turn my shit into something special. So, what I share with you now is just my own life results from my own life experiences, and what I've done to find peace and enjoy success on my own terms.

Once I had posted my blogs and videos of my ultrarunning and my thoughts, people began approaching me in person and online to say that my lifestyle had inspired them, and they loved how I was living and what I was doing. This meant such a lot to me personally. I'd spent years of nobody ever believing in me or accepting me without a beer or a loud crowd, but it was all different now. I was living my passion, peace, and purpose.

The best asset I have is my mental self-reliance; I believe in personal freedom, and that peace comes from a person's individual mind. When we correct the mind, the body follows; it may take a lot of time, but that's the way it is.

My diet becoming plant-based and vegan helped to take my life to another level. And I opened up my food journey online, as I wanted others to share this amazing state of mind and being. It's phenomenal but not popular.

Remember back in April 2013 when I ran the marathon of 26.2 miles, untrained, at 19-and-a-half stones, wearing a tracksuit and hillwalking shoes? I spent a lot of time alone in the mountains and hills before that race, just sitting with nature, healing, meditating, and preparing my mind for what was to come. Through meditation and healing, I decided what I wanted to be, and worked every day towards it.

I couldn't catch Mo Farah or these other amazing athletes over 5k, 10k, or the marathon, but endurance is my thing. Running offers different distances for all different people, depending on their strengths. My physiology and lack of years of training means I will never break the world record at the marathon. But at ultra-marathons I could finish high up, as it is more psychological in this sport, and that's what attracted me. A sport where the better you think, the stronger you become.

When you correct the mind, the body will follow, so that's why it's all been done so fast. I worked on the inner game, and the mind was corrected long before any step forward was taken. The foundations are solid, and that's why I recommend meditation and a library to anyone wanting to get fit, because to be emotionally fit will win over any short-term solution in the long run. Emotional fitness makes you outstanding time after time.

I chose to put all the belief into myself on the journey, in order to benefit the life around me. I'm doing it all again, but on a different level now. I've made peace with my family and old lifestyle and friends, too. Over time, I have changed my environment, situations, and even the desires I once had.

Where I live, people are not peaceful, calm, or promote eating raw fruits and vegetables. The area is a built-up, agitated, and anxious society of loud clubs, sports stadiums, and an idea that happiness is the opposite of inner peace.

Society bombards us with many advertisements of happiness, but to me it's all about your own rules for happiness. Mine is that if I am breathing, with an opportunity to live, then I am happy. The expansion of that happiness comes from mental peace, a life of contentment, wellbeing, and joy that I can share with others. What's yours?

If you rise in the tough times, then you will dominate in the good times; it's all about progress. If you want something in life, then work at it. That's what I've been doing with my life, and I have education and a sporting life in place to continually grow from and add value to others. I choose to run and live like I do now, rather than go to the pub with my old mates.

We all have choices, and our life is about the effort given to what we want to focus on.

For centuries, Scotsmen have gone to the pub to talk and philosophise about life, but I want to be a good role model to my daughter through my lifestyle, and that environment does not match my picture of how I want to set an example.

People say I'm talented now because of what I do, but it has nothing to do with talent or luck, it's all down to effort and going internal. I was told in school that I couldn't run, and I spent my youth with nobody believing in me or my abilities, so I became a rebel and I never understood the power of effort.

Now I believe in me, and I have the chance to express this. The only thing that follows work is results. I share my story online and in my blogs, not to tell others how to live or what's right or wrong. I share my journey and story to show that transformation is possible, life is possible, and it's all down to you changing that story you tell yourself of why you can't run 100 miles, why you can't lose 5 stones in weight, or why you can't ask out someone you fancy at work.

I don't know what's right or wrong in your life, but I share my own story to show that nobody has it all good. It's just that some of us get up and go for it in life, with effort and work on the inner world. And that's it. It's down to effort, so learn to stay focused and always believe in yourself. Correct your own mind towards your own goals, is the message I want to send out.

I am an example of what I believe is possible. I believe in health, self-reliance, and inner peace. I believe you can rise from any adversity. All humans have inner power and we can use any pain to push ourselves forward, build a life and lifestyle where we can become our best self, and share that with all those around us.

Now that I've done what I wanted to do in life, I'm building on times I have had with my daughter, building on my times with friends, meeting new people, spending time on education and growth, building on my fitness, nutrition, and lifestyle. I will never stop growing now. By continually learning and developing myself every day, I am valuing myself and then I can give to everyone around me. Becoming the best version of myself means that I become the best father I can be, and the best person to be around for others.

No-one can put that effort in for you; no-one can run your miles, do your press-ups, read your books. It's all self-made from the effort you have inside, and it's in every one of us if we look. We are more powerful than we think and can do a lot more than we can imagine.

Chapter 7

With lots of character-building experiences, running and amazing times 2014 had been a great year. I was invited on national TV, which was brilliant and a great platform to share my passion and lifestyle with others. I was featured in newspapers up and down the country, several magazines, and won nice running prizes. Being recognised for my efforts, I was also given free running shoes and help with clothing by two major sports brands, to help me on my forward journey.

I ran lots of marathons, a 35-mile ultra, the 100-mile ultra marathon, and enjoyed a lovely trip to Amsterdam with my mate Wallace, which showed me a different lifestyle. Looking at Amsterdam through the eyes of an athlete was very different to my previous visit.

As I was nowhere near hitting a Personal Best on the course, I decided to take my shoes off near the end to really slow down the experience. This allowed me to walk around the track to the finishing line, just taking in the atmosphere and surroundings and appreciating my life and the experience. It also allowed me to appreciate the new friends and teachers I have found in books and online, who have helped on this journey forward.

As a young kid from Glasgow, who was told by secondary school teachers that I couldn't run and being left out the football team, I now felt free from the limitations of my past. Think about it for a minute: how would it feel going across the finishing line at the Olympic Stadium in Amsterdam for someone who came from where I did? How do you think running around a packed stadium in peak health, after being in a foreign mental asylum, would feel?

When I went out running through Glasgow city centre at 4am, on my own, wearing my headlamp, people would scream at me, "why are you running?" and "do you not take a day off?" I would just smile, laugh, and think to myself that I used to be in those crowds and questioning people who were different. Now I have become the one who is different and I question the crowds. In my experience, the crowds never seem to reach smart decisions together.

Conventional wisdom is almost always wrong; they once said the earth was flat! That's why I am more drawn towards independence, self-reliance, and personal development. I do compare myself to others, though. But now whatever I see the crowd doing then I usually do the opposite, and that's what has brought me the results I have today in life, health, and ultra running. I choose my own peace before somebody else's weekend party.

On social media I was told by others that I might be able to run 9 minute miles all day long in training, but that it wouldn't do much good on race day. I was also starting to notice some changes in the runners around me. There was a different attitude to what I was doing and more criticism, yet nobody had bothered before tv, newspapers, and sports brands started to help me.

When I was the fat guy at the back just completing challenges, it was always fun. Then I got into the middle of the pack, where there's less talking as you run. But when I got closer to the front, people started saying all different things. It was even suggested that the sports brands were helping me with my clothes for an ulterior motive, and that I didn't deserve to run marathons because I had spent time in prison!

I didn't listen to these comments. In my opinion, the sports brands were investing in a guy with nothing who had invested in himself. If anything, that illustrates that helping me gives encouragement for others to try out the sport, put in the effort, and get rewarded. But when you do well, just like in old times, some people will question, criticise, and say whatever they can to stop your progress.

If I stopped to answer all of the questions and criticism, then I wouldn't be where I am today. It's better to be a selective listener; listen to people with results. Deep down, it's always better to be respected than liked by others. Being liked today is easy; everyone gets 'liked' on social media, but to be respected is a different feeling altogether.

People were now looking at me as competition. My resting heart rate, at 33, was showing signs of what I could do at the sport, but I am way beyond other people's competition.

Instead, it's about sharing a message of health and recovery, even redemption. I don't do it for the competition, I don't need anything external to motivate me to do what I do with my life. I meditate and take care of myself for me, but if people see me as competition then that's their perception. If they don't beat me, it's not my problem.

I love my life and what I do. I value and love myself, and I've filled myself up with that love to share with others. I've faced death, so I am hardly going to be fussed about another human being looking at me as competition on a running field or in the city centre. I just do what works for me in life.

I decided that I would run an event every week for a while to prove that my diet of fruits and vegetables was working, and once again people said that I couldn't. Everywhere you go in life people will offer unsolicited advice, usually with no results of their own. So, who they are trying to convince? If you want to do anything in life, find someone who has already done it, see what they do, then do the same thing, and see how it goes. Having role models can change your life.

On YouTube, I looked up a guy called Michael Arnstein, who is a fruitarian. I sent him an email then went off to try it out and prove to myself that the diet works. Throughout January, I ran 702 miles over the ice and snow. People were saying that to get results I would need to do speed work. The funny thing, is I never discussed running while I ran, it was more about philosophy and life change, and a focus on health more than structured training. I did briefly try a running club; the people were great, but running talk is not that interesting to me.

Although I run, club running is the last thing on my mind, and I was turning up for speed work after already having run 20 miles. They couldn't understand my running, and I couldn't understand how much they made a big deal of things.

I reverted to running with nature. If I'm with people, then it's nice to communicate while running and to enjoy the lifestyle, but running is really just my peace with nature on foot. I don't see it like it shows on TV; it's relaxed and fun. If I was going to be a better athlete then I needed to learn the part that the other athletes do, but I preferred to stick to my slow pace and high miles in training, then just run fast on race day.

I was having fun with new friends I had met, running around the mountains, clocking up high miles and new adventures, and it was great. I was no longer doing it for the events. I had just fallen in love with the lifestyle, the process, ultra-running, the health, the food, speaking, sharing, writing. Everything I was doing was a reminder of why I started, and it all made sense to me.

I wanted to be the best dad and example of a human being I could be. But when you openly say you're vegan in a meat-eating culture, or that you don't need to drink alcohol because you are happy without it, it doesn't always go down well. People don't like you questioning them, never mind raising the social standard. People feel threatened when you change the way they see the world. I don't need any animal products to be an athlete, but there are athletes all over the world who are vegan yet it's not publicised much on TV. I recommend searching 'plant-based nutrition' in YouTube or Google, and you will see the likes of Serena Williams and Brendan Brazier.

With the food changes, my body was undergoing physical changes – muscles popping up, strength increasing, recovery being faster, and running becoming better and better. But it's the mental benefits that matter most. When I am eating raw fruits and vegetables, I don't experience what other people call stress. I believe stress comes from bad nutrition and being upset with life not matching your pictures. But with real food, you have a real-world view and the nutrition in your system cuts off the stress. Cutting off stress with healthy foods and a healthy lifestyle then pours into all other areas of life. And without stress, mental illness and most physical illnesses cannot be fed. So, your mind, body, and spirit starts to bring out all the best parts of you as a human being.

To say food changed my life, would be an understatement. Food changed my mental health, my physical and also emotional fitness levels, to be able to set higher standards for myself and to have the courage to take life on in a new way. I could now answer the critics with results, but also to show that mental health recovery is possible, life change is possible, and that everything in life gets better when *you* get better. My message for others was simple: eat the apple, meditate, read the book, have a nice sleep, and enjoy your life.

By this stage, I knew I was going to hit a sub 3-hour marathon with ease, and I knew I wouldn't need the training plans or rest that others did. I was going to race every week, not rest, and still experience life and results on a diet of fruit and vegetables. Show time!

In the first race of 2014, I ran 33 miles up in Aberdeen in 4 hours and 1 minute; a warm-up event of what was to come. In April, I took on the challenge to run the Glasgow to Edinburgh ultra-marathon – 55 miles. Like most runners, after the race I shared a blog to share the experience, and recorded reaching my highest ever position in a race.

For me, the ultra-running life just keeps getting better and more adventurous. Every experience is different from the last, and it's a great time to be around like-minded people and at the same time learning a lot about ourselves individually. Endurance teaches us a lot in life, and I think that's why I love the sport so much; it's character building.

The Glasgow-Edinburgh ultra was close to home; from the city where I live, along the canal route to Scotland's capital city. Online, there is a great ultra community where people share results, lifestyle, nutrition, and blogs about the experience. Mark – an English guy I met through the Facebook ultra page – was doing his first ultra, so I said he could stay over at mine before the race. I had space for more people, and as my house is round the corner from the starting line, it made sense.

Although I've had a fast life change and experienced great results in running so quickly, I wasn't taking the race seriously. I was sticking with my plan to go around courses to get experience, learn the sport, meet the people, and plan for the future along the way. At that stage, I'd only been running 24 months, so I really appreciated being amongst great athletes and inspiring runners. I compete with myself and try to be the best I can be. Others constantly tell me how I can do, what I should win and so on, and it would be easy to get an ego from that, but I utilise my ego the same way I utilise my life change... I aim to be the best I can, with good health, lifestyle, performance, and compassion.

So, back to the running. At the start, Mark and another of my running friends, Wilson, were ready. As I looked around the course, I saw some familiar faces. Roly, who I've met on a few runs so far, is a role model of how I want to be later in life with running. The same with Robert, who I knew through strava (an online app that keeps track of running activities through gps). We joked at the start, but he gave me some pointers that I tried out, like having one less bottle on the race vest as I'm running at a faster pace now. It made sense and worked a treat.

I saw a few other friends — Carrie, who I met at the D33 (a 33-mile race in Aberdeen), and who is pretty inspirational; and my mate, Chen, who I see everywhere, too. Their photographs of life really stand out.

I usually meditate and relax before a race to focus, but through experience in ultras and running I'm always focused now and it feels great. I took off at 8 minute miles and less for the first half, which I did with Roly, talking away and laughing. We were joined by a girl called Izzy, who was pretty inspirational, not because of what she has won but the adversities in life she has overcome. That's something else I have noticed about the adventurous life-style; behind the strength of character and the results, there is a time when suffering and hardship is overcome by mental toughness. And that's maybe something we all share in this sport but also in life itself. Before I go philosophical again, I'll get back to running...

At Checkpoint 1 (at 13 miles), I just had water. During the race, we are allowed to leave a bag with food and drink at a certain point, and I had put mine at Checkpoint 2. I always pack a lot, because mentally I have the comfort of knowing that if I get hurt then I can hobble to the end with a picnic rather than drop out hurt and starving. If I'm going well, I just leave all the food and drink for others.

By Checkpoint 2, I was feeling great. I had some of these Naked bars to try, and ate early in the run for a change, so just picked up almond coffee, an Alpro plant-based yoghurt. and took a few spoonfuls of papaya & some strawberries. Then off I went, caught up with Izzy again and found Roly was back. We enjoyed a few miles, taking information about competing from Izzy. As the miles went on, she said I could push on, so I did, and picked up the pace.

I overtook a few runners and reached Checkpoint 3 laughing, but not stopping for long. I just had some water and was off again. As I picked up the pace, I was feeling strong. After 30 miles, I reached for the dates which I'd been fuelling with in recent weeks, but there weren't any. I'd forgotten to pack them!

Instead, I took some almond breeze coffee, which sends me bonkers on race day because I don't have caffeine in everyday life. Some runners have cola, gels, or some sort of caffeine, but as I don't take any products which use fish, I prefer to take almond breeze coffee as I know it's natural with the coffee stimulant. My pace was dropping, although I was still overtaking more runners, but I needed food.

At Checkpoint 4, there didn't appear to be any vegan food. The cakes and flapjacks didn't show their ingredients, so I just grabbed a handful of nuts and went off again. I was still feeling hungry as I hit Checkpoint 5, and knew I had to eat something. So, I ate the flapjacks and off I went; the boost of energy from the food helped me to finish the race strongly in 5th place.

This had been another new experience, with lots to learn from, including that taking coffee gives a high and a low. So, finding the right foods and fluids is definitely key at ultras. As I don't take coffee, Naked bars, Lucozade, or even Alpro yoghurt in daily life, all the stimulants affect my sleep for the next day or two and knock me off-balance from my plant-based way of life. But it's something I know to expect, and the results in running and races show me that it's working.

I was needing less on race days now, felt lighter on my feet, and was becoming disciplined at pacing. And at the age of 29, my last 3 races saw me finish 1st (at 10k), 13th (33 miles), and now 5th at this 55 miles. More importantly, I was amongst great runners, athletes, and people in an amazing community, and was so grateful for the opportunity.

I felt happy in life, having found my place, my peace, my passion that I can share with so many others. Even now, I'm in love with the process and the journey, and every day look at ways to get better.

My friend, Robert, finished 1st in 6:51, the girl Izzy was 1st lady just behind me, and I was in 5th place in 7:45, Roly came 14th, and it was just a great day. At the end, a girl called Sarah offered me a free massage so I got my feet done, as my legs felt fine. I'm more into meditation than massages, but maybe I'll try all of that in the future. I just don't feel I need it just now.

I headed home to Glasgow and had food at the Flying Duck on my own, as I had missed the vegan event which was on. My mates, Wilson and Mark, enjoyed every part of the ultra and also finished together, and we met up back at my house for a few cups of tea and a good chat about the whole experience.

When they both left, I went to bed just thinking: this is living, this is my ultra, and I'm really enjoying doing what I do, for myself, for others, for my family, the animals, and for the whole lifestyle.

Chapter 8

The week after that race, I won a local 10k race in 37:11, after running 6 miles to the race start and another 6 miles to get back home. The following week, it was time for the Manchester marathon.

This time, I was more experienced and more focused, and ran a steady planned race, using the watch to keep the pace of every mile. It was a beautiful day and I felt at ease, comfortable, and relaxed, and managed to finish in 2:55, being cheered across the finishing line by a few friends who I had met on the journey. We celebrated with tea and a good chat then I headed back home to Glasgow to start my preparations for the Hoka Highland Fling race.

The Highland Fling event is a 53-mile trail race which takes place every April, and follows the route of the West Highland Way, Scotland's oldest official long distance foot-path through the Loch Lomond and Trossachs National Park.

As I had been racing every week for quite some time, some people were thinking that my legs must start to tire soon, but they don't understand the food choice of raw fruits and vegetables, and how it works. Here's a blog I wrote about the Hoka Highland Fling 2014 to share my message:

The Hoka Highland Fling, Scotland's most packed ultra-marathon with around 1,000 runners from all over the world and 53 miles of scenery, trails, lochs, mountains and the freedom of Scotland under your feet. I had run my first sub 3 marathon in 2:55 at Manchester the week before; before that, 55 miles Glasgow to Edinburgh and came 5th in 7:45, along with a negative split at a 33-mile race; and a 1st place finish at a 10k.

The running has been character-building. I've been so strong, disciplined, running a lot and having the time of my life, so I'm sure an ultra will eventually take the wind out my sails. Would it be this one?

I started with my mate, Barry; he had a plan for the race. I didn't have a clue where the checkpoints were and didn't study the course at all, but I like that. When it's easily marked, there's no need for a map. Just run in new places. I've run the first part of the West Highland Way before, and a few miles at Rowardennan, and feel at home around Ben Lomond but that's not part of the route (the mountain beside Rowardennan trail).

It was lovely to meet so many people at the start of the race and throughout; people who have inspired me, have been friends, and I'm glad to be a small part of this large community.

I made a video of what I would eat and how I prepare for ultras, and put it onto my YouTube for others. I was trying out some normal food (the packet food that the majority eat), gels, and bars, so would this be good or bad? Time and miles would tell.

Off we set at a pace. I like to start from behind to get a feel for the task ahead, but Barry was eager to get going so we set out at 8:30 minute miles and got faster. First checkpoint, with no worries and feeling strong, we met lots of friends along the way and had great chat about adventures, what's next, and what's for today. On the trails, people don't talk about celebrity gossip, TV news, and city life; we share things about each other and it's a nice connection, it's a beautiful lifestyle.

So, onto food... Instead of using dates, at first I decided to use bars and gels as I'd be running the West Highland Way in 8 weeks, and food was going to be important. I'm open that I take coffee at ultras. It's a major stimulant, and I never realised how much it messes with the head until I stopped drinking it in daily life a while ago. I know coffee is from plants, but it knocks you off your head. It's a major energy boost, but with that boost comes the come-down, and most people rely on it again and again. After an ultra, I need to wait until the coffee comes out of my system completely now so that I can sleep properly again.

So, feeling good, talking around the field and catching up, on we went to Conic Hill – the hill that everyone talks about as being tough. I like a challenge. Barry was with his mate, Del, from the club, so I went a climb. Guys were asking if I was doing the relay as I went up fast. I overtook a few people, and that mindset was creeping in: I'm here now, so why hold back?

Then downwards I went, fast into Balmaha. I was at the aid station waiting on Barry, and he came in and told me to go on ahead. Marshals say don't wait on people, too.

Off I went, with the hunter's mentality again, pulling the finishing line towards me and unfolding the scenery into my mind – the moments, the air, and nature, with mantras going in my mind: a fool seeks happiness in the distance and a wise man pulls it under his feet.

I love the whole journey and embrace it. I pull it under my feet and I keep going past people, having a talk and laugh with.

Then another aid station. I picked up some fruit and a lettuce hogie, as I share in videos. My mate from previous races said he would rather put pins in his eyes than eat the food I had, so I replied with., 'Enjoy your pins then!' It's fun eating fruit and vegetables, and the banter is fun, too. I saw many people along the route, and just kept going.

Then I had some peace to myself. I looked at the lochs, and started to sing. I don't listen to music when I run; my heartbeat is my motivation. But as I was singing, my leg got locked in rocks and I went over on my ankle and hands. Bruised, hurt, and dazed, I got up *laughing. I said, 'What a plonker!' to myself, but now it was time to get up and get on with it.*

It was my own fault for coming away from the moment to sing, though, and probably the reason why I don't listen to music (lack of concentration of the real moment). The character-building time was here. I needed to suffer again, as it had been a while since I had. But here it was, so what did I do? What did I think? How would I overcome it?

I was dazed and hobbling, got to Benglas Farm, and thought the aid station was there, but it wasn't. I'd read the wrong sign. This wasn't Benglas. Dazed and zapped with energy (comedown from gels and coffee, I believe), I was having words with myself. I reminded myself of the journey, the past, and a wee quote from the film Braveheart: 'It's all for nothing if you don't have freedom.' So, one step, one breath, and it was time to bring out the mental toughness, 'finding fuel in an empty tank'.

A few people overtook over me, but I got to the checkpoint and got strapped up. They asked if I wanted a doctor, but I said I'd see one at the end. I knew nothing was broken, so off I went, grabbed a bag of dates, and ate them all. It was time to get back to natural; time to fuel with some plant power.

I looked to the side and there were calves having a feed from their mother cow; further on, baby lambs with the sheep. I started to pick up again, bringing all the thoughts to why I do all I do. I run to be a better me, for my daughter, family, friends, strangers, and the animals.

I overtook people again, with one of the guys congratulating me on my comeback as I passed.

I pulled my phone out of my bag and texted my mate Danny to say I'd be finished soon, as he was waiting on me. Into the finish, and I heard the bagpipes. I had the emotions of freedom and independence that come from this sport, this lifestyle, and those bagpipes. Scotland will always be my home.

Laughing through the journey, I headed onto the red carpet and finished in 8:36. My mate Danny said I was close to the top – 17th out of 1000 runners, I think. A fast time over the hills and rocks, and a character-building journey. Everyone along the way always comments on me smiling, but after the life journey I've had, how can I not smile? How can I not have fun pushing myself like this and overcoming adversity? I love when it's hard, because I live a peaceful life now with balanced foods and great health, so the ultras give me the chance to feel every emotion again, like a roller-coaster. And after the race is over, I get off the ride and back to eating good food, keeping hydrated, meditating, and sleeping well.

So, I run to suffer, to overcome it, to become and keep becoming a better me, to look into the journey, to have peace in the moment, no matter what feelings there are in the moment. The ultras remind me of the feelings I have of strength, power, and the whole life journey I've been on. I'm grateful to be part of this life, I'm grateful to share, experience, and just give the best I possibly can to this life. This is my ultra. This is our ultra.

A fortnight later, Danny and I went to do the Kintyre Way ultra. We went two miles the wrong way, stopped to help an older man who fell off his bike, and were separated near the end of the race. But I still managed to get into second place in the race, with the winner, Stan, running a fantastic race and beating the course record with 15 minutes or so. I was only two minutes behind the course record with my time. Running, life, and everything, was going well, and I was on TV again, too.

Lots of things that people don't see get left out in quick articles, like meditation, reading, and studying. As with anything in life, people are rewarded in public for what they practise for years in private. It may look like quick results on the outside, but if you cut to the core of any person, the key to their success is all in the daily routine; small things done well over time.

Chapter 9

I have a nice house beside the canal now, with a room for my daughter when she stays over. Before I became a father, I was a different person, with a different mindset and with different goals and desires in life. The reason I am all that I am today is because of my daughter coming into the world and looking at me as a role model, a father, a person with deeper meaning. There is not a day that goes by that I don't thank her for her being alive.

I didn't want my little girl growing up thinking her dad went to a pub or nightclub and didn't bother with her. That would only encourage her to go to the same places when she was older, to see why they were more important than her time with her daddy. That's what we do as kids: we grow up and look at our parents' lives. We are all either warnings or examples.

So, with the lifestyle I live now, I know if I'm old and grey and my daughter is trekking some mountain, travelling and being free, she will enjoy the feelings her daddy did while he did the same. My example is one of freedom, and that's the opposite of control.

I'm not doing it to prove to the world that I'm good enough or for people to accept me as a dad. I am doing it because I love it, and for the people and places it has brought into my life. I enjoy running, and love time with my friends, too. What's 60 miles now? 60 miles of deep talking, planning, and support between friends – blissful.

Friends like Dave, Danny, Iain, Barry, and Wallace have helped me more than they could know by simply being there, following their own ambitions and dreams. I've met many new friends, with people supporting me in my community and on social media. Some who were strangers at the start of the journey helped me and have become my closest friends, opening up my heart to new personal relationships and a deeper meaning to life. People like Debbie, who just gave me pointers at the right times. There are so many people to thank. Nobody does it on their own; when you go different places, you will meet different people, and they are amazing.

In my youth, I was brought up in a goldfish bowl, but the world has 7 billion people in it today (and that's not including the animals), and there is so much out there to experience and live, it's all down to what you focus on. At first, I set out on my own, the solitary path to the mountains and meditation, but then it created a new lifestyle over time – new people, new connections, and new experience of living life this way. Looking at my daughter when we are together makes me realise that I am now living the life I envisioned and planned – to be her dad, in the best health possible, and with a lifestyle we can share. It takes all of us to make a community, a country and a world; nobody does it on their own.

With all the life change, the results, the media interest, being on tv and in all the national newspapers again, I received many heart-warming and open messages from people privately and on social media, which made me see that all my efforts had been worthwhile.

Other people were now looking to running, to sport, to life change, to food, a new direction. So many people were tuning in and taking the positives from my story; often, they could see themselves in me. I think suffering is one thing we can all understand, and overcoming it is one thing we can all do by making peace or progressing.

It hit home when a young boy I watched grow up saw my story in the local paper and then took a new direction – taking exercise, eating healthily, and getting fit. I met him in the park, all grown up with a girlfriend, and he said he had changed after seeing my story. His gran sent me a Facebook message, saying something had just clicked with him after reading about me the paper.

Maybe the world has too much information these days, too much of telling people what to do, think or believe. Maybe they just need more inspiration by life examples. People who walk the walk and talk the talk in their life, and that's all I aim to do. I love speaking and connecting to people, but I listen a lot, too.

All the publicity and all the people connecting reminded me of the strangers who had helped me on my path. I had been alone at one time, yet I was now helping strangers on their path. Life has gone full circle.

In life, we get caught up thinking that our friends are our teachers in life, and we make friends due to proximity, who we work and go to school with, or meet at a social event. But a teacher, a role model, a speaker, someone who has found a way out of no way – that's what changes lives. That might be someone you need to find online, or in a book.

Your friends are needed for comfort, but they are not made to be your teachers in life. I learned that I needed to look outside of my environment to find people who could help me progress and grow as a person. I looked at Anthony Robins, Jim Rohn, Eric Thomas, Greg Plitt; the list is endless. I knew I wasn't born to just entertain people at a party. I knew there was something deeper to me, and the more I gave, the more I got, and the more people changed things in themselves, too. By me changing in myself, it had a ripple effect.

I genuinely believe everyone has greatness in them, but they need to step away from average, comfortable, and normal, to progress. Be willing to do more than average – everyone will change in life, but progress is a choice.

Reading a book a day isn't normal, running 100 miles isn't normal, or playing a piano all day isn't normal, but if you love it then why not? Why not you? Why not now? Look within your own heart and mind, and open up your song with the world around you. If you love playing music, then play. Don't just to go to a bar to sing someone else's song on a Friday night just to fit in. Live your own passion from your heart, and share your gift with the world.

If you like art, then paint. If you like writing, then write. Writing has been a passion of mine for years, but I was never any good. Even online, I was corrected for my grammar. But I knew I would write a book one day. I had no idea how, but I just knew why, and that if I kept on doing it then it would happen. Fail forward rather than fall back on something you can already do… and progress.

Out of the blue, I met a lady called Sheila, who has written and published her own book called *Happiness Begins With You*. She heard me speak at a seminar and we met for lunch, then she put me in contact with an author group where I met my publisher. Being around others who write, and working with an editor to correct my spelling and grammar, is how I've managed to get this book to you now. It's amazing how people do help you when you know where you are going and what you want.

I started this journey with nothing but an iPhone, running shoes, and an idea. Now I have a laptop, and am a member of an author group. When I give public talks or meet new people, they always ask me, 'Where is the book?' Truth be told, I've been so focused on doing all I can in the 24 hours given that I've never thought about structure, business cards, or plans. I've just focused on passion and adding value to others around me with the tools I have available.

It was my mission to be the best I could for my daughter, the animals, and everyone I've met on the journey, and that has taken my time and focus until now. But this book is now here as a message. To say that whatever you want to do in life, just go and do it and enjoy they journey.

It's not about what you do when everyone watches, it's what you do when nobody watches. Who are you then? When the chips are down, which you shows up? Just as it's not what you eat 20% of the time that makes you have less energy, it's what you eat 80% of the time; it's not what you do from 9-5 that makes you who you are, it's what you do 5-9 that determines everything. It's what people don't see that makes you who you are.

When you are *you*, then be all you can be. And when you get to the goal outside, you will realise that the goal was never the important part, but the journey itself and what sort of person you have become along the way. Then it's all about what you can give by becoming more of yourself.

There are so many labels I've been given in life: prisoner, sectioned mental patient, well, healthy, athlete, public speaker, inspiration, and now author. But really, my name is William Robertson and I thrive by adding value to life. I've even given a talk to psychiatrists in Glasgow, speaking of mental health recovery and using my experiences as an example. I also spoke at the SECC in Glasgow at Vegfest, about transformation and life change through food and emotional fitness. I don't put limits on life; it's all about love, growth, progress, having fun, and then growth and contribution.

In my culture growing up, the sport of running was for the upper class, and ultra runners would be considered crazy. But in reality, it's a very sane and natural sport of sober enjoyment with nature. The only reason TV crews filmed me ultra running was because of my example of craziness; finding peace was very unusual. Why else would major sports brands sponsor a guy with no gold medals? It's so unusual that I've used my mind and made a lifestyle from doing the simple things over and over again which others just forget to do, like eat the apple, drink water, read a book, meditate, sleep well, and do the opposite of what the crowd does.

Every success book gives you the same advice over and over. When other people my age went to the gym to get ready for the beach, I went to the library to get ready for a lifestyle. The life experience, added to a passion for communication, on-the-spot coaching, even public speaking and getting around amazing people, has helped me to progress to a new level of living and deeper understanding.

I'm not doing anything magical, just the simple things. The best advice I could ever leave behind is that it's not who you know in life, it's *what* you know... and then, what results you can execute with what you know when the time comes to show it.

Showing is always better than telling. In the words of Jim Rohn: 'Success is not something you get, success is something you attract by the person you become.' We can all become more at any time; we can all be healthier, fitter, stronger and, most importantly, we can always love more.

It's not the fault of the weather, the government, or your ex-partner. It's not the fault of the world around you. We

are living in the best of times, with technology, with educa-
tion, and inspiration levelling the playing field. It's all out
there for you to become all you can possibly be.

In Scotland, grown adults complain about everything
from the weather to the tax man, but they could up and
move to a new country at any time. They're not trees.
Everyone has freedom in the UK – the freedom to go to
the park, or the library, to pick a career of their choosing, or
a college course, a new diet, a lifestyle, a social gathering.
We have the opportunity of choice in the country where I
live and in a lot of other countries, but people don't want
that sort of truth given to them because it takes away their
excuses.

In the same way, information doesn't help people half as
much as inspiration. Everyone knows how to be healthy,
yet so many people in Britain are overweight! That's
because people need inspiration; they need people around
them with results. In the modern world, everyone is throw-
ing around facts and figures, but you need to be on guard as
to what goes into your mind, because it has a major conse-
quence on the person you become.

But the one thing you can't measure is your self-worth.
My story is just one of millions of people who understand
that your biography is not your destiny; your choices are.

Some Thoughts on Nutrition

When your inner world is out of tune, it's not an illness –
it's bad nutrition. And hopefully this book can add more
value to the time you spend looking at what you eat. If
you are stressed, would eating strawberries, raspberries,

coconuts, and pineapples, and drinking water help? Take time to read into the subject more. Look at your own choices – time, fitness, health, lifestyle, and who has got you eating and drinking what you drink now, thinking like you think, who gave you the world view you have, who chose what holidays you celebrate, what animals are to be eaten and what ones to be pets, who told you all of this, and when was the last time you made your own decision about your lifestyle.

To talk about nutrition change, you need to talk about a person's childhood. In India, for example, they have rice; China, they will have noodles; Mediterranean countries, they eat a lot of fresh vegetables, and they are all trim, healthy and fit. Yes, they might have fish and some animals in their diet, but in many cases over 80% of the foods come from plants. So, it's not what you eat 20% of the time that matters, it's the other 80% that determines the quality of your physical, emotional, and mental health.

I'm sure even in my home country of Scotland, people used to eat home-made soup, potatoes, and bread rather than the food that's been put in science labs to get people addicted to a product in marketing plans.

At the moment, there is a big government focus on cutting down on sugar. White sugar is made in a lab; real sugar comes from fruit, and it's not solid like you see in packets. The sugar you see in a packet is a product not a plant, so never think that the fruit you have in sugar is the same. Packaged sugar can knock you mentally off balance, and when you are off balance inside then it shows outside.

Have a look at the people around you. Why do you think they make the choices they do? Who is in the moment? Who looks calm? Who is having deep conversations and connecting well to their environment? Who wouldn't want to be fit, healthy and active in this life? Young kids love to run as soon as they can walk. They have adventures and love to be with animals.

The word vegan has also been marketed a lot now, with all the sugar products and substitutes, which is great for the animals. But vegan doesn't mean healthy. Vegan simply means you don't eat, hurt, or wear animals, and that you choose that lifestyle. What I've learned in my culture is that people use the word to play the moral high ground or to stand out as different from others, which I'm not against but neither am I for it.

Vegans can eat cakes, drink beer, and do all the other things like smoke drugs and follow the hippy lifestyle. But, for me, it doesn't make sense to help all the animals yet hurt yourself in the process. True health begins with yourself. It's like the warning when you travel on an aeroplane: put your own oxygen mask on first in an emergency, then you can help your children to put on theirs. Health is a serious matter to help people with.

I believe the diet that makes sense is simply human food for human people. Monkeys and elephants don't get sick like humans do, or spend half the year with the cold and flu for being outside. And you don't see Doritos or hamburgers growing on trees in loving environments.

Humans don't crave things when they are healthy; they create a lifestyle and become free and the best version of themselves.

When I became vegan and totally cut out everything else, and then moved on to just a plant-based diet, it made me slump at first. I lost energy and really questioned myself and what I was doing. Initially, it was difficult. I grabbed the chocolate Oreo biscuits and they made me sick. I had no idea what my body was doing but I just knew it was right; it was like coming off drugs or alcohol.

At first, all I was eating was porridge with soya milk in the morning, pasta and tomato sauce, banana, apples, oranges, water, and tins of fruit put through a blender. So, I headed to the fruit and vegetable shop in my area, explained that I'd gone vegan and didn't know how to cook vegetables or eat healthily, so could they help? In Glasgow, people enjoy banter and we laugh a lot in conversation, so we laughed together, the staff handed me a book, and a new journey began.

My choices were then unlimited. Adding in spinach, kale, broccoli, carrot, and sweet potatoes gave me an extra boost, along with adding a daily smoothie with hemp, wheatgrass, spirulina, chai seeds, flaxseed and nuts.

My recovery was now happening faster, my energy was boosted, and I had a spring in my step. In 2013, when I became vegetarian, I dropped from 21 stones in weight to 15 stones. I went vegan at the start of 2014, and ran a marathon in 3:11 – a huge drop from 4:53.

I was then running a marathon and an ultra-marathon in the same week, recovering faster and feeling stronger. The more fruit and vegetables I was eating, the better I was feeling every day, the more alert I became, and my mental health changed a lot.

Recovery is all about living a good life. Now I was living the ultra life, which means beyond normal, and with my foods being as natural as my running. I never want to go back to 'normal' food or lifestyle ever again.

Then I watched Michael Arnstein and Brendan Brazier online, along with Doctor John McDougall on foods and performance, and off I went again. I added in watermelon, pineapple, papaya, strawberries, blueberries, cherry tomatoes, cucumber, and high water content fruits into my diet, along with green smoothies, and ran 202 miles in the same week.

I was indestructible now, and my weight dropped to just over 12 stones. I was flying, so signing up to the 100 miles quickly made sense. I knew I could do it, no matter who told me not to. I could write a bigger book about the people who told me to stop, or don't do this, or criticised. Some even said I shouldn't be allowed the opportunity to run after being locked up, but I used that criticism to lace up my shoes and enjoy my beyond-normal life, bringing new ideas and examples to those who looked into my journey online.

Once 2015 came, I was racing every week, my mental focus was alive, waking up at 4am every day, reading books, and taking my whole life to another level. I believe in fruits and vegetables, and I believe that the tortoise can win the race in the long run and live the good life. I believe in the fairytales and dreams of life, and why not? I'm living proof of it now, and sharing a story of transformation that many others can do, too.

I love success stories, but my favourite stories are about the person who messes everything up and gets their life back together again. And that's what I set out to do: to be my own hero and share this one day in the best way I could.

This natural food and change just made sense to me – simple raw fruits and vegetables bringing the best physical, mental, and emotional health for the journey. In the morning, I would start with a banana smoothie and soya milk, chai seeds, flaxseed, wheatgrass, hemp and sometimes goji berries. Then I would just eat as much fruit as possible.

In Britain, people see fruit as 5 a day, and having one portion. Yes, I made sure I had the apple a day, but I would eat lots; I'd eat the bundle of bananas, the packet of tomatoes, the full pineapple, the full watermelon, papaya, packet of strawberries, blueberries, and so on. Because people are marketed by tv, they see fruit as one piece or a smoothie, but if a human passed a blackberry bush or an apple tree in the olden days, they would have eaten as much as they possibly could. So, that's what I do.

With fruit in the UK, there is a myth that it's expensive, but the reality is that people have been marketed away from their local fruit shop or fruit market or wholesaler. I was getting a box of bananas all the way from Costa Rica for £5, which is roughly about 10p for a banana.

Nobody in my old life runs 100 miles or has a resting heart rate of 33, and I don't need to point that out. I just laugh with them and say that food and lifestyle is all about choice. This book is aimed at helping you see that health can be mocked and laughed at, but if you want results in health and lifestyle then you personally need to take it seriously… for yourself.

The salad bars at buffets and restaurants are always freshly prepared in the UK and most countries I've visited, and around £3-£5 (or cheaper abroad) for as much as you can eat. You don't pay for tap water in Scotland either, so eating this way didn't just make more sense, it made me look at finances differently. It made me healthier, study more, be different.

Choose health, and look at things differently, as it can put you on a new path in life. The best insurance you will ever get is your own body and mind full of fruit and vegetables.

Why not? Why not you? Why not now? Be as healthy as you can, as wealthy as you can, and as focused as you can, to set new goals and aim for some higher purpose.

At night time, in my culture everyone needs cooked food, but the healthier you become the less it's needed. I now add in bread, pasta once again, rice and beans – in burrito-style, like they do in Mexico – and I'm creative with food and just enjoy the natural life. Around 80% of my food intake is fruits and vegetables, the rest is nuts, seeds, rice, grains, and bread. If I'm out with my daughter or friends and there's a vegan dish we can share, then I will go for it. Why not try a few of the simple recipes I use, which you can mix and match, and see how your feel?

Morning: banana smoothie, as much fruit as you can eat, drink water, enjoy tea, porridge, healthy cereal with no cows' milk or honey. For iron levels, try out pumpkin seeds followed by some oranges, and that will save you putting iron tablets on your health bill. With these foods, you are aiming to keep yourself well. Invest in yourself!

Afternoon: if eating out, then salad bar, carvery without meat; try Mexican or even Subway, if you are on the go, maybe hearty Italian bread with the salad only. Jumping into eating just fruit at the beginning might be a bit much for you, after having years of addictive foods in your diet. But keep adding in fruit, as the more good stuff you add in, the more bad your body will start to leave out over time.

Night: boil rice, mix in vegetables, carrots, peas, spinach, lentils, beans, and a sauce of your choice – either made with your own tomatoes, herbs and spices, or buy a pre-made sauce – mix it all up and serve with fajitas. Pasta without egg or dairy – check the packets and play detective – and add to your own sauce or something pre-made. This will get easier and a lot of fun when you get creative. Chinese noodles and stir fry are good; have a look at any supermarket now and it's all there and available ready-made. Once you see how it's done, you can make your own. Cook in soya sauce and just enjoy yourself.

Food is fun, and if you type 'plant-based' into a search engine, the world is waiting to give you all of these foods. It's not marketed a lot because it doesn't make money, but now you see lots of people with a nutrition book. I'm speaking from going from 21 stones on a bar stool to an athlete on a podium within 24 months, due to my food choices and mental toughness training.

I feel phenomenal, and I want that option to be available to everyone. I know the options have always been there, but when I was brought up, eating watermelons and pineapples was not common. The protein word was shoved down the throats of anyone in fitness, yet I believe I'm fitter than people who take these things and I've been training less time. My resting heart rate is 33, and I'm living a good life. I don't say that to brag; I'm saying it to explain that lots of people will push products to help their financial wealth, not *your* health. But you can make your own choices and do your research and your health will benefit.

Remember, I don't have any talent or athletic background; the teacher never picked me for the football team, because I couldn't run; my family genetics are all arthritis and early death; a few years ago, doctors told me I had a deranged liver, inflamed stomach, and resting heart rate of 86. But my food choices have helped me to take my marathon times from 4:53 to 2:55 and I'm just getting started, while others have tried for years to break 3 hours.

People from my old life always ask if I don't miss those old times. But if you saw the sun rise and the stars at night the way I do now, if you could see life through my eyes, then you would only look at drink, drugs, TV, and the other entertainments as a distraction from moments in life for which you want to be fully present.

I would never be the man I am today without my daughter looking at me that day and helping me to find a meaning to my life. I believe that things in life happen to prepare us. Now I am home, in the city where it all began, with new memories of travelling and running and meeting new friends all added in.

The real journey in life is to find unconditional love for those in your life.

Finally

I've been reading books on success, the rich, economics, finance, and investments, in order to help me to be free financially, and so that nobody has to look after me in any way.

I was invited to Barcelona by a brilliant businessman and public speaker, Art Napolitano, who offered to pay for my flight tickets if I could 'hop over' – and I immediately said yes. I had no idea what I was doing, but knew that this was a path I must go on in life now, away from just ultra running, fruit and vegetables, and a life with nature and peace.

I would learn fast that business and city life is a cold, dark, and lonely place when you don't have a team, a plan, or a strategy, but I got the flight and met up with friends I had met on Facebook, and had a great time taking in the business world in multi-cultural Barcelona.

Up at 4am, morning run, 6am no smoothie, no breakfast, coffee-and-go with no nutrition and working at a seminar, meeting new people, networking – it all takes its toll. Mapping out a city, the underground, and travel, through trial and error rather than with a plan, I was confronted by pickpockets but kept my hands at my side, looking them straight in the eyes with a book by my side. I knew what the youths we're doing. I'm streetwise and there's no books on that; it comes from having lived that life.

I learned that travelling alone on the road to success in the financial world is as tough as the 100-mile running journey; it's an inner battle of mind, body, and spirit. I'm 30 years old and know how to set goals and achieve them. Maybe it's my childhood that drives me; maybe it's past pain, past hurt; maybe it's just my mind always wanting to learn and expand.

This time, I knew it was a journey like no other, and on the flight home I noticed a change in me. It was like an inner shift, an alignment of seeing money as a magnet rather than a piece of paper; more like a goal and a hand, rather than something that pays the bills.

The value you bring to the marketplace is where you will earn society's better fruits. As you hold this book in your hand, it has a price tag, it's trade, it's value. But I had spent the last few years of my life adding value and forgetting the money.

After reading Napoleon Hill's *Think and Grow Rich* and also *The Science of Getting Rich* by Wallace D. Wattles, it's turned me into a hustler in a new way, rather than just a guy who shares blogs, goes on tv and radio, and runs around eating apples, sharing his deep part of life through YouTube, and providing free content. People pay more attention to what they pay for, according to the books, yet in my world the best things in the UK are free – nature, mountains, art galleries, and libraries.

And this confusion ended up in me being sectioned again.

My mind began twisting as I arrived back in Glasgow. I heard a clicking noise, I'd had no sleep, was full of coffee, no proper nutrition, and had tried to outlast the sun by working on myself to get into the business identity. Arriving back at my house, I heard every click on the phone, on tv, or even outside on a fire engine or looking up at a plane. I felt everything was connected and that life was going through me. What about the bad stuff? Who does that, the terrorism, the heartache, was the world war not won by a clicking and tapping noise? I wanted peace to meditate and relax, to be in my house, but I was fighting sleep.

I put my running shoes on and went out of the door. I'd no running watch as it was out of battery, still wore a Barcelona wristband, and was thinking I was a walking click-clock in the stock market. I told myself that as long as I had myself, my passport, a dollar (which I got in New York before the twin towers went down), then I would be okay. But as I ran around Glasgow, phrases ran through my mind like 'Smile every mile' but I just got more depressed. I wanted peace not to smile; I wanted sleep not chatter. *What was that clicking?*

I decided that if the clicking was me, then the world could do without me, so I threw my iPhone and house keys into the River Clyde. In my mind, I thought that if I'd done enough good then the world would put me back together;

if I'd done bad, then I was dead already because success without fulfilment is failure.

I needed into my house, but I had no keys and I wasn't going to kick my own door in. I didn't want to talk to the police, but ended up wandering into a police station, looking confused. They gave me water, spoke to me, reassured me, but all I wanted was to be locked in a cell to have some peace, or for my front door to be put in by the police so that neighbours wouldn't think I'd been working with the police and governments. That's how much the mind can play tricks on us.

But why the tricks? Lack of sleep? Nutrition? Lifestyle? Lying? Yes, lying. My success in recovery and lifestyle change all came about when I stopped taking medication. It's something I've been hiding from the world. Paranoia is what kept my mouth shut, and continuing to read.

After phoning around, the police got hold of my sister. She gave me a cuddle, but I was cold, hurt, and lonely inside. Maybe these were all the classic signs of someone who would commit suicide but there was no chance of me jumping off a bridge. First, I've not got the bottle to do that, and second, I've got a little girl who calls me Daddy, and I have a promise to fulfil to her. My why was what was keeping me breathing; my why was going to put me back together now that I'd lost my way!

My sister took me to my mum's, but all I wanted was sleep. I was in my 'mind house' but wanted to be in my own house. The tv noise was soothing my mind, but then doctors arrived at my mum's house and I started losing my mind. Why were they here? What was going on? The doctors I knew left, saying that I'd be okay with some sleep; other doctors were trying to give me medication. That's the last thing I wanted! I saw the stuff as poison because I'd stopped taking it and my success and freedom lifestyle was a result of choices, not medication. But nobody knew that secret except me.

Two days later, I felt trapped. Naked, I locked myself in my mum's living room and started writing on her walls. I wanted out. I didn't want to take that medication. It was like the scene from *Braveheart* when William Wallace spat out the pain relief; that's what I did with the medication, as quotes ran through my head.

No more messing around. The police arrived and put me in handcuffs, naked. I was sectioned and rolled into a police van with a blanket over my head. I've been in these situations before and always managed to keep calm by reading signs on the back of the van. But with no sleep, psychosis was surely part of my reality now.

I hadn't slept in two days in my mum's house. In hospital I was sedated, jagged, held down, and they said later they almost had to knock me unconscious as I kept shouting 'Freedom!' In my mind, there was still clicking; my words were real, my life was not. I didn't want to be dead, I wasn't suicidal, I wanted my freedom away from doctors, the government.

Psychosis can be deadly; some people never recover. My recovery was fast, almost life-changing. The doctors put it down to medication; I put it down to sleep and rest.

But now I'm complying with medication. Why? Because if I can take myself off it and be successful over time, then who's saying I can't do it by complying and working with the doctors, psychiatrists, and therapy over time.

I believe in personal development. I believe the mind is a muscle, and I also believe we are all more powerful than we think we are and can do a lot more than we can imagine. In one of Tony Robins' seminars, he said that when the bumble bee goes after its selfish pursuit of nectar, pollen is spread along the way, creating flowers. Everything is connected, and I believe that, too.

I'm leaving this book on this chapter; coming back after a second section, showing that I'm human. As my daughter's mum said, 'Even Superman had to take his cape of at times.'

I've given my soul out there publicly, now it's time to rest up and take time out. Through these tough times and 30 days in hospital, I meditated more, relaxed, and built a relationship with my daughter's mum, and we are all moving forward together as a family in a new and deeper connecting journey.

I've no idea what's next – business, lifestyle, family, the stock market, or what you are going to do after putting this book down. But I do know that the human spirit and life itself is a beautiful thing.

Everything has its place in the design of life and, with freedom being a state of mind, we can all have the power of that choice, regardless of where we stand now in the modern world.

I wish you good luck!

Contact details

twitter : @wrobertson4am

email : wrobertson4am@gmail.com

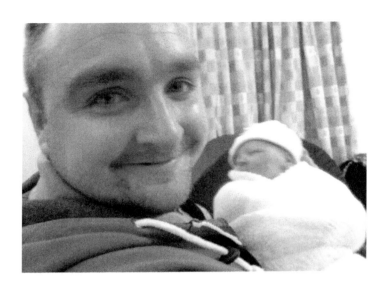

Lightning Source UK Ltd.
Milton Keynes UK
UKOW07f0335140817
307258UK00006B/18/P

 **ANCHOR BOOKS**

A CLASSIC COLLECTION OF GHOST STORIES AND MINI SAGAS

Edited by

Sarah Andrew

First published in Great Britain in 2001 by
ANCHOR BOOKS
Remus House,
Coltsfoot Drive,
Peterborough, PE2 9JX
Telephone (01733) 898102

HB ISBN 1 85930 924 0
SB ISBN 1 85930 929 1

FOREWORD

Anchor Books is a small press, established in 1992, with the aim of promoting readable poetry to as wide an audience as possible.

We hope to establish an outlet for writers of poetry who may have struggled to see their work in print.

The poems presented here have been selected from many entries. Editing proved to be a difficult task and as the Editor, the final selection was mine.

I trust this selection will delight and please the authors and all those who enjoy reading poetry.

Sarah Andrew
Editor

The Ghost Dog

on page 39.

Written by

Susan Carol Robert.

CONTENTS

SANCTUARY

He lay prostrate in the chancel of the church.
Scurrying feet sounded outside. A dog barked.
Surely he was safe here!
'Oh God - don't let them put that white sheet over me
and stone me to death,' he whispered.
But it was too late - the brass rubbers had arrived.

Peter Davies

ONE CAN WONDER WHY

Robin Hood and his men robbed the rich to help the poor. He and his gang were considered outlaws. Yet Third World governments, *acknowledged by the West,* can legally kill, imprison or starve people, forcing them to leave their country. They, in turn, come to the West and are called, refugees.

Leslie Holgate

1943

Do I remember the war?
Course I do. Two years old
tin chamber pot pulled
well down over my head
running to the air raid shelter.
We'd sit and listen. 'Mum
can you hear that Fokker?'
Gran: 'No need for that language
my gal.'

Ivan Langham

ONE DREADFUL DAY

Up Sunday morning to make the tea, the pain began unexpectedly.
The pain got worse, I dialled 999, the ambulance took him away.
The operation started immediately, too much blood was lost.
They tried to help, but all in vain, he died at 3pm.

Valerie Ann Bellingham

LADY VIOLET

Passing the haunted castle, Lucy paused,
darkness suddenly descended.
Lucy was lifted up and looked down on a
beautiful lady followed by a horrible man
wielding an axe, cold was intense,
then she was lowered.
Sadness overcame her, she shook violently
still trembling she exclaimed, 'Lady Violet's ghost!'

Bessie Groves

A LEMMING NAMED HOBSON

Hobson broke away from the horde
racing towards the cliff.
'Why should I jump off that cliff just
because the others want to?' he said.
He walked away, proud of his independence . . .
until he reached a lovely, quite deserted cliff.
'This one's *my* choice!' he exclaimed,
leaping merrily over it.

Charles Lawrence

MY GREAT AUNT'S HOUSE

A ghostly round head
Looks up at a walnut tree
Oblivious to motorway construction
Traffic, and the cries of executed
Geese, rats and mice run among rusty
Ploughs and tractors.

Paul Wilkins

ONE COW

It was 5 o'clock and Lewis still wasn't home from school. I was
beginning to panic as I got on my bicycle and hurried down the road in
search of him. We were new to the area and I soon realised that I'd
taken the wrong turning. Halfway down the long isolated lane I came
across a small cottage set back from the road. 'I'll ask the way,' I
thought. It was twilight as I banged on the front door. Receiving no
answer I peered through the dusty window. In the corner of a dark room
I could see what looked like the glimmer from a tilly lamp, so venturing
round to the rear door, which stood ajar, I knocked and entered. In the
dim light, I could see the floor was earth, a small fire flickered in the
grate. It was sparsely furnished and in a chair by the fire sat an elderly
lady with a crocheted shawl around her shoulders. She rose to greet me.
After giving me directions we chatted as she followed me out. Putting
my hand on her shoulder, I asked if she was alright.
'I'm fine,' she answered, 'I still have one cow left.'
I was back home by 6 o'clock and my young son was already home
safe. The next day I returned to the cottage with a basket of food. On
entering I found no one, just an empty semi-derelict house where mice
scuttled and spiders knitted their webs.

Jenny Anderson

LOST

I was in a dark hole trapped in a castle very ancient trying to escape but no avail.

I spotted a window but it was too high. I cried loud for someone to hear me. I saw a shadow.

I heard the sounds of keys coming towards me.

I took the key and reached for the window and escaped to safety.

F Walles

ACE-HIGH

Every muscle ached now. It needed a
superhuman effort to keep going. Strain
showing in face and body, heart racing.
The arm rose again and contact made.
It felt good - it was good.
Above the tumultuous applause the voice
of the umpire could just be heard -
Game, Set and Match.

B Williams

TOMMY'S GHOST

The door opened, a grey shape appeared in the doorway; from his bed Tommy watched, he awoke as the door creaked, his heart was pounding in his chest, he clutched at the bed covers and watched through slit eyes.

The shape moved further through the doorway wavering slightly, it didn't have legs but appeared to glide above the floor, as his eyes grew accustomed to the darkness Tommy saw that it had eyes that glowed in the dark room, its mouth was huge and contorted in a silent scream.

Tommy shut his eyes tight then opened them again, to his horror it was still there, it was either getting bigger or it was moving closer, gripping the bedclothes he could feel a scream building up inside him.

The thing was moving closer to Tommy's bed, he could almost smell it, its mouth was moving but no sound was coming out, it raised one grey shadow-like arm and reached out towards the bed.

Tommy couldn't hold his scream in, he opened his mouth but to his horror no sound came out, he released his grip on the bedclothes and flapped his hands at the hideous shape that was now leaning over him, trying to push it away, his hands just disappeared into the grey mist, it wouldn't go away.

'Morning Tommy, time to get up for school,' his mother's voice came out of the mist, opening his eyes he realised with relief it was all a bad dream.

Marcus Tyler

STORM FORCE

Sally and Neil on their way home from school, satchels on their backs,
chatting.
Sally was eight, Neil was ten and liked football.
'Try to get it from me,' he said; she tried, laughing, and missed.
Suddenly, a violent thunderstorm erupted, black clouds, then thunder
roared.
'What's that?' asked Sally.
'It's thunder, we are going to have a storm.'
'What's a storm?' she asked.
'It happens after a heatwave, the heat builds up, then explodes.'
Lightning flashed across the sky.
'What's that?'
'It's lightning, we must take cover.'
The heavens opened, rain came pouring down flooding the gutters.
As they ran down the road, the wind howled.
'I'm frightened,' said Sally, 'are we going to die?'
'No, nothing like that, we'll sit in the shop yonder.' The door was
closed, half-day.
They huddled together as the storm roared overhead, hair and clothes
soaked.
'What's happening Neil?' as Sally began to cry.
'Don't cry Sally, it's a natural phenomenon, and if we were at home in
the day, we would watch it, it's so spectacular.'
Suddenly it ceased,
'Come on Sally, let's go home.'
They arrived home, drenched and scared,
Sally said to her mother, 'Mum, we were caught in a natural
phenomenon, I thought I was going to die.'
'Not unless you stand under a tree,' said Mum.

Wendy Dawson

Do Ghosts Have Christmas?

It was Christmas Eve and not a word had been spoken when little
Jimmy asked his father 'Dad, do ghosts have Christmas?'
His dad laughed. 'If you're thinking of old Ned, he's such a stubborn
old coot. I should not think he has much joy.'
Just then an icy wind flew through the house. All the doors, they banged
shut.
'There I told you, still up to his old tricks.' Ned was the ghost that came
with the house. No one had seen him but he was heard all over the old
house. Some say he was a past owner who did not take to visitors. His
Dad said it was old Nick himself. There were no photos on the wall,
each time they hung something up, old Ned would throw them across
the room.
'Maybe he wants a present?' said Timmy. 'That old pipe of
Grandfather's would make a good gift for him.'
The room was suddenly warm and quiet.
'I do believe you're right,' said Dad. He fetched the pipe from the old
trunk in the hall, 'Here Ned, Happy Christmas.'
From that moment on, not a sound was heard of Ned in the old house.
Maybe now and again you might see the smoking pipe float down the
hall.

Colin Allsop

COVERT AFFAIR

How would he react at this latest meeting? Would he be pleased to see her?

Could they keep up this charade of not caring for each other. Because from prying eyes, their affair must be concealed.
Knowing in the days ahead, there would be precious time to spend together.

S Mullinger

SHE CAME IN THE NIGHT!

The phantom came in the village of Brackenhurst at the time of Michaelmas, but Angela Braithwaite laughed when shopping in the local supermarket!

Angela bought Edgington Hall, a very impressive house, standing in its own grounds and as she stopped her BMW red car at the large thick oak door, she grinned all over her pretty face. I've seen nothing sinister in the old house and I have abided here for two years!

Living in the Lord of the Manor's home, Angela was somewhat disliked, for the Lord in his day had ill-treated his wife well-known in the village, the grapevine regulars kept the knowledge well-oiled.

After a cricket match some thirty years earlier, the Lord of Edgington Hall, William, saw his wife Ellen talking excitedly to a very handsome young man. Jealousy afterwards ruled the day and Ellen was never seen again in public, the rumour had it, that she was kept down in the cellar of the old house and those who dared to potter around the old Hall at night, heard her disoriented cries.

Ellen's funeral took place on an afternoon when thunder and lightning was at its worst and old crone Sarah Hampton believed she saw the coffin jerk en route to the cemetery, it was Sarah who told Angela of the phantom at her home.

Angela went to bed as usual. She never thought of it being Michaelmas.

At midnight, she was rudely awakened to find Ellen by her bedside screaming *W-i-l-l-i-a-m!*

Alma Montgomery Frank

SIGNED AND SEALED

The postage stamp
to determine
The delivery
of the letter,
The contents
has the power
to change lives,
A still moment
to read and digest,
To have
or not have,
It's true,
A winner,
Rags to riches,
Let celebrations begin!

Margarette Phillips

THE SILENTS

The silence was calling to him. During the lonely furthest-from-sunrise hours of the cerement-wrapped night, he could hear the whispering non-voices beckoning, beseeching him to listen to their dark secrets, buried deep in shadow.

Insistently, the tomb-silent cadences writhed sibilantly inside his head, scurrying like a million black bugs into his ears, in time with the blood pounding in his brain. Blood that was spat out by his lurching heart. He scrutinised the darkness that threatened to smother him, a mosaic of tarred ravens stitched within a sable shroud, but he could see nothing. Yet still they summoned, coaxing him into leaving the safety of the covers.

Through no effort of his imagination could he envisage the appearance of his unseen, unheard tormentors, that preyed upon him in these gelatinous hours. The ticking of the clock served only to incite the silence further, as though it knew but a few hours remained until daylight freed him. Often had he left a candle burning. But the tremulous flame merely flung more shadows across the low ceiling, that scuttled like spiders into the corners of the room, where they watched and whispered.

Abruptly he awoke, to feel in the darkness his fears crawl, slither and haul themselves along his tender body. He fought frenziedly, but was swallowed whole by the sensuous lips from which the silence dripped. He tried to scream, but the whispering poured into his mouth like thick, dark ink.

And then there was silence.

Jonathan Goodwin

A SPECIAL LOVE

We laid your earthly body in the ground to rest.
We said a prayer and then we left.
At home I knew you were waiting for me.
A time for cake and a cup of tea.

As I opened the door I saw you there.
Sitting as usual in your favourite chair.
Your smile said 'Welcome' as I came in.
The world was whole and mine again.

As I wandered through our home that night,
The moon cast shadows that seemed so right.
Then scented perfume filled the air,
Your favourite shampoo as you washed your hair.

Sunlight sparkled on the dew,
Our garden which was fashioned by you
Seemed to come alive once more,
As I saw you standing by the door

It seems that I am on my own,
But I know that I am not alone.
You're there, you're everywhere it seems,
My love, you're even in my dreams.

A ghost, a spirit, but I don't care.
I know My love, you'll always be there.
And when my time on Earth is done.
You'll be waiting for me at my Father's Home.

E Timmins

THE ISLAND

After sailing for many weary days, they
finally reached the island. It was a
peaceful paradise of plenty, where food
grew on trees and fish swam like jewels
in a sapphire sea. They marvelled at
the scarlet songbirds and the sparkling
sand, feeling that they had found rest
at last.

Rebecca Nichol

THE CRUISE

The large yacht sailed into the Mediterranean. I was with three girls
invited by the owner.
We arrived in port. My three friends rushed onto the quay.
The boss called me into his cabin. He was naked.
'Knickers off, or leave!' he glared.
I rushed out after the others.

Keith Murdoch

WELCOME GHOST

Angela saved a five-year-old Alsation from being put to sleep. They enjoyed a wonderful life together. He made it his business to guard her wherever they went. When he passed away, Angela was so distraught, she could not think of getting another dog.

In every possible way, Angela missed her companion, especially at night, remembering how he slept in his basket beside her bed. Every now and again, he would touch her with his paw to assure her of his constant protection.

For years, Angela had taken turns to help an elderly couple in the evenings, get them to bed after preparing their supper, and had always taken Laddie with her. He gave them added pleasure.

She was also glad of his company and protection on the lonely walk home. She continued to help the couple after Laddie passed away, even though she had become afraid of being alone. One particular night a strange male walked towards her, and her heart stood still with fear. How she wished Laddie was by her side . . . suddenly the man was almost upon her, and she fully realised by his movements that she was in grave danger.

Then she felt and saw the ghost of her beloved Laddie by her side. He sprang at the man who must also have seen what she did. He screamed and ran in the opposite direction as fast as his legs could carry him.

Angela knew she need never be afraid again. Laddie's ghost would ever protect her.

Madge H Paul

IT'S NOT ALWAYS THE WINNING . . .

I hadn't wanted to enter the race but my trainer insisted I was in great form. I saw the hurdles and blanched, but jumped them effortlessly. Running up the final straight I felt the merciless sting of the whip. I threw my jockey and sailed on regardless. Horse-sense prevailed.

Adrianne Jones

THE ANGLE GRINDER - AWAKENING

The mist hung over the town like a shroud. Young men pulled their collars tight to their necks and hoped to keep out the damp. Footsteps echoed on cobbled streets lit by lamps which shone their light like orange pinpricks through the veil that enveloped this deserted suburbia.

Children dragged duvets over their heads and listened to the pant of their frightened breath. Suddenly a chilling shudder went down their spines as in the distance a high-pitched scream reverberated along the valley and met in reply a soft moan from the wind.

Even over the noise of the television set the shrill cry was heard by mothers and fathers who looked at each other with fear in their eyes.

Couples embraced even tighter than usual and clung to each other for dear life. Dogs paced up and down frantically, yelping with fear then cowering with terror. The town lay silent like a ghostly liner on collision course with some phantom iceberg.

All was still, even the sighing of the trees was frozen in a hush.

Old women prayed to God and rocked quickly back and forth in well-worn armchairs, old men sat scared remembering a time when sunlight lit up the valley and death was a never-never land, hidden from view by the long summer days of youthful adventure.

Now the time had come. The Prophet hadn't lied, their sin and greed would bring judgement and vengeance. Tonight the cold sweat of fear had consumed the hope of grace and mercy.

The Angle Grinder had been awakened . . .

Francis McFaul

A SHADOW

When I move it's there, large and small, follows when the day is bright and never makes a sound, disappears when the sun goes in, but is often there.

A shadow.

Margaret Upson

THE GHOST OF THE VILLAGE GREEN

It was late December and the sun was sinking fast, and six children were setting off across the village green past the old graveyard when they heard a horrible scream. *Shriek! Shriek!*

It came from the direction of the old mansion on the hill. A place children would go, peer through its cobweb-covered windows, listen to its creaking doors, rattling windows and watch mice playing on its bare wood floors. Then the winter sky darkened, thunder roared and lightning lit up the sky. Could it be an angry ghost of years past? The children ran and screamed for above the trees, bare of leaves appeared the witch, her twisted face highlighted by the lightning, while her shrieking prompted groans from the spooky graveyard.

Unafraid of thunder and rain or rivers of water rushing from the hills, washing away the fence keeping cows, sheep and pigs from straying, the witch shook the big black crows from the trees. Both wind and wild dogs howled sending an eerie chill through the air.

All seemed lost when out from the shadows came the friendly ghost of winters past, and in fear of her life the wicked witch ran away. Never looking back.

The ghost can be seen in December when the moon is full, children singing and skipping behind him.

No tracks of either children nor ghost were ever found, no wonder because this is the story of little Johnny's dream.

Maurice Hope

The (Holy) Ghost Busters

It was dark and eerie as John and Peter made their way home from the disco. The music had been vociferous and non-stop.

It was pleasant to slope off into the cool night air. They glanced up at the church clock, which informed them it was five minutes to midnight.

They were now passing the churchyard gate which swung invitingly open on its hinges and drew their attention with a dry squeak which pierced the clear night air as though inviting them inside the silent graveyard. John's attention was aroused, his hand shot out to grasp Peter's sleeve. How about a bit of ghost busting, he suggested? Peter became a willing partner. They edged their way through the gates and along the path lined with gravestones. An owl greeted them from its vantage point, its presence camouflaged by the dense leaves of the yew tree. A rat scurried across the path making its nocturnal journey from one source of food to another. In this otherwise tranquil place, the old elm trees interrupted the silence as the gentle breeze moved its leaves and occasionally let out a sigh as one branch rubbed against another.

They were now close to the church door. Was that a flickering light they could see? With trembling hand they tried the door, to their surprise it yielded and revealed a porch. Peter fumbled in his pocket for a torch. To his surprise, this door was accessible. First a crack revealed the dim interior illuminated by a single candle glow. The door opened wide, revealing a good number of people. As their eyes grew accustomed to the light, a voice struck up shattering the deathly silence!

Praise God from whom all blessings flow, Praise Father, Son and *Holy Ghost*. Peter directed the beam of his torch towards the notice board . . . *Saturday Night Prayer Meeting, Come And Go As You Please.*

John Waby

THE CAR CHASE

The man in the car was ramming another vehicle. I over took them. The woman's face was a picture of terror. I hooted my horn to attract his attention pulling alongside. We both stopped. The other car disappeared. I pointed my rifle at his face. I drove off very satisfied.

Raymond Fenech

THE RUNE STONE

With an oil lamp at the thick of night he crept up to the stone and tried to read the runic symbols inscribed thereon. The wind howled and lashed at him as though it were outraged by his presence in that place, but he fought against it. Nothing was going to prevent him from discovering the truth.

A hidden cave nearby held his captive - the weird woman who lived on the outskirts of the village. He'd watched her for months and always it was she who came here with her flowers, mumbling and chanting. Then she who claimed her rune stones had given her a message for the priest. Always the message was of a soul he should pray for that had passed over in violent circumstances. Always no one had discovered the body until she pointed the way.

He'd found her here that morning standing before the stone holding a bunch of white roses as an offering.

A rotund moon watched him drag her from the cave and throw her to the ground before the stone. He would have the truth from her, whatever the cost. Quietly she got up, raised her arms and began chanting.

Rain fell. Thunder rumbled and lightning pointed at him. His screams were lost within the angry crack that struck him like a sword right through. He fell.

The rain ceased and the thunder rolled away. There would be no more bodies now. He was gone.

Kim Montia

AN ORDINARY VILLAGE

As I reached the little village it seemed to me to be quite ordinary. Just like a hundred other villages throughout the land - a typical quiet English village on a lovely June day.

I had soon walked the short distance through it and came to the beautiful little church, which I decided to visit.

Outside it had been sweltering but inside it was pleasantly cool, the atmosphere, though peaceful and quiet, somehow felt strange. I picked up a leaflet describing the church and started walking around examining the features and taking photographs. I read on - Founded in the thirteenth century . . . magnificent pillars . . . box pews . . . four bells in the tower, several interesting memorials, fine wood carvings and a beautiful chancel screen which seemed so exquisite that I took several photographs of it before leaving.

Some days later I took the film to be developed and anxiously awaited the time for collection hoping that I would get some good shots of the church interior.

At last the day arrived when I collected the photographs and excitedly I studied them in turn. I was not disappointed, each one was turning out well, I had captured the features I wanted until I came to the last photograph.

I could not believe my eyes and my heart seemed to stop beating momentarily, then continued pounding, for there in front of my eyes in the first two rows of that empty church were two lines of hooded monks, clearly seen kneeling in prayer!

Terry Daley

FATE

Marc lay critically wounded from the car accident, he needed blood. His group was rare. Computer data was searched. Only one match, two states away, the donor unavailable. A porter heard and came forward. Surname the same. Marc was saved. They talked later, Marc had found his long-lost father.

Duchess Newman

ABOUT TO FACE BATTLE

I am a brave knight about to face battle
Armour tin and rattle
Sword twisted, shield about
Wondering what this fight about?

Galloping horses' picture seen
Stride every step there's ever been
No blood will there ever shred
If every prop is ever read.

He rises to the ring
He strikes, he hits
His mind full of dreadling tricks.

Jay

HAUNTED CASTLES

An old castle ruins
Full of charm, mysteries
Darkness falls. Eyes
of fear. A cold chill
up my spine.
Footsteps, strange
banging, no explanation,
lashing storms.
Ringing bells
Shakes the castle
to rubble once
again.

Alan Hattersley

DID THE CLOCK STOP?

Sarah opened her mail to find six white candles in one of the parcels, she was quite pleased to have them come so quickly as it would mean that she would not now run out. Just a she started to open another letter the telephone rang again, this time it was June her friend who was crying over a row that she had had with her husband yet again, over him staying out late drinking. Around a quarter of an hour she sat this time, which meant she had to leave the rest of her mail until that evening and rush off to work. After having her tea, she set off for her flower arranging class, as it was just half past six she had got half an hour before it started. On walking back to her car once it had closed for the evening, she thought she saw Andrew walking away fro the car, yet as she got to it he appeared to be nowhere. Upon driving home in her car she noticed the clock had gone funny again, this time stopping at half past six. On opening the front door she noticed the telephone was ringing again, it was June crying again as she told her that her husband had been run down by a hit and run driver at around quarter past six that evening. A quick glance at the wall clock told her that it had stopped at half past six.

Keith L Powell

First Term

The mission had been a success. The troops had been assembled and their rations distributed. The whistle was to be blown for the second time that year, and it was about to begin . . .

As the sound echoed through the hall, the students filed out of Assembly, chattering excitedly to their new classmates.

Helen Marshall

SPITTING IMAGE

After tracing his father, only to find he had died two years ago, John had decided to visit the woman his father had lived with for the last thirty years. The woman agreed to his request and a meeting was arranged.

Finding no one home John sat in the rocking chair on the veranda and chewed tobacco, spitting occasionally into the shiny spittoon which rested on a circular mat. The view of the mountains was spectacular, 'good choice old man', John thought to himself.

He sat there for two hours, feeling the wait would be worth it, to hear about the rest of his father's life, since he had moved when John was thirty-nine.

Just as he was spitting another glob of tobacco into the spittoon a car pulled into the driveway and crashed straight into the waste bins at the side of the house. John rushed quickly to the vehicle but his assistance wasn't needed. The woman got out and smiled at him,
'Hello John, you know, you're the spitting image of your dad,' she said 'and you gave me a bit of a fright there.'

After that they talked for hours and John stayed at the house overnight, bringing his family with him on the next visit.

Danny Coleman

Wrap Up Warm

Tap on the cabin door.

'Get up Miss. Put on warm clothing. Here's your life jacket. Go up on deck.'

Bewildered 'What's happening,' she doesn't remember seeing that steward before.

Suitably clothed, clutching life jacket and handbag. An elderly gentleman with a large moustache is by the stairs.
'On your own? I'll look after you.'

She had been on this cruise a week. She hasn't seen him before. It feels cold too. But it's August. They had told her New York would be hot and humid at this time.

An officer. Not one that she recognises.

She's dreaming, that's it. She notices a large clock. It's nearly midnight. Strange dream.

It seems to take them ages to get outside. It normally takes ten minutes. She's timed it.

The elderly gentleman is fussing about her. Hasn't he heard of women's lib?

But it is very cold.

On deck her gentleman says he will find her a boat. Stay right there.

The officer moves to starboard. She can hear him shouting orders over what sounds like steam hissing.

She sees a group of people, suddenly everything is silence except the hum of the ship.

The people break up. Come towards her, several she has seen before.

A woman says to her 'It's 2.20. We are members of a Titanic society.
This is near the spot.'
'We were observing a minute's silence for the brave souls,' someone
else says,
'Who are still being heroic,' she whispers.

Melanie M Burgess

A MISUNDERSTANDING

We quarrelled last night, he rang this morning begging me to meet him.
'At the bridge,' he said 'I'll wait till noon, then I'll jump.;
I must go to him, he needs me. I ran frantically, but I was   he'd
thrown himself over.

'Twas his first bungy jump.

Gladys Baillie

ῙOST DOG

Ῑer was sick in bed
῀na was particularly bad,
ῗked my sister and I
ong the garage for our dad,
῀ on our coats and ran along the street,
῀ past the gap in the fence, to go into Peggy's field,
A῀ ῀en we saw, a mist, afloat, an unreal but moving smog,
and in its centre, an eerie large shadowed dog,
We were both scared, and into Peggy's field we ducked
we hid down low, the air was cold,
it crept upon our skin until the cloudy dog went past,
Its head was taller than the garage roof's,
and when it got to the top of the old pit road,
We frightened girls ran to, and hammered on dad's garage door,
Dad opened it and asked us, what we were frightened for,
we told dad, he put us in the garage, then locked the door,
He went to look, seeing nothing, dad took us home quick,
when we told mum, we were both still shaking, I felt sick,
Mum said years ago there had been a very large puppy
born on the farm, and when it had grown,
The dog had jumped the fence and got out,
It ran up the old pit road, to the top on its own,
Just as a lorry came round the corner
and knocked the large dog down,
Mother remembered, this story mum told,
About The Ghost Dog from the farm, that walks the old pit road.

Susan Carole Roberts

THE PROMISE

She had promised to yield,
sate his needs, tame his hunger,
their eyes met?
She was no tease he was certain,
coyly she inclined her head,
he followed fascinated
to the small door.
Flushed with heat she
suddenly revealed all!
Gasping he lunged forward!
laughingly she surrendered,
his favourite dinner.

Ivy Wood

THE GHOST

One dark evening I decided to pull my peas for tomorrow's dinner. I am a widow living alone. I was in the garden when I saw a man looking at my garden.

'Who are you?' I said.

'I am a ghost. Don't worry,' he said.

I've never seen a ghost before. I felt frightened.

'I'm sorry,' he said ' to frighten you. I just want to see what vegetables you have.'

Then he disappeared. He must have flown away.

Next day I went to pick the peas, but they all had gone. I decided the ghost had taken them. When I told my friend she said

'Don't worry, ghosts don't appear in the same place if they know they frightened you.'

One day I was shopping in town when I saw my ghost looking in a window. I was amazed and said

'What are you doing here?'

He said 'I'm sorry I am no ghost. I took your peas because I was hungry and out of work, but I am starting a good job next week. By the way I didn't fly away from your garden, I hid next-door behind bushes.

He asked her to have coffee with him, which she did. She invited him to tea. Eventually they ended up married. One day she called him saying 'There is an old man waving to me in the garden.

He looked and said 'That's my dad. He died eight years ago. Now we must both believe in ghosts.'

K Taylor

Mini Saga

It was 1991. We were in a queue in the Lenin Mausoleum, Red Square having been to the Lenin Museum.

Suddenly, when I was facing Lenin, the Guard was given an order. The queue stopped. I was pushed forward. Would they shoot? No!

The KGB wanted me to see Lenin.

Nola B Small

STABBING PAINS

Katie and Emma were tucked up in their beds. The clock struck
midnight. Katie opened her eyes slightly then rolled over pulling the
covers over her shoulder. She glared at Emma's bed. Her heart stopped.
She tried to scream but no sound would come out. She didn't know
what to do. She pulled the covers up over her face, so only her eyes
were showing. She tried not to make any noise, but her heart was
pounding making her breathing heavy. She watched the white manly
figure standing over Emma, with what looked like a large knife, raised
the knife and stab it right in Emma's side. Katie squeaked pulling the
covers all the way over her head, thinking 'go away, go away'.

The next thing she knew the sun was shining and Emma wasn't in her
bed. Katie thought she must have been dreaming.

She went downstairs to find her mum comforting Emma, as Emma had
bad stabbing pains in her side. Katie stood as white as a sheet with a
lump in her throat, thinking 'no it couldn't of been real, could it?'

J Cross

A Short Story Entitled Scenarios

I dreamt of you last night. We were running across the park, and you ran ahead of me. You'd got your wings.

It was a dream. It may have been a nightmare.

Simon Morton

FINAL COUNTDOWN

Five minutes to go!

We lay in bed; the baby, blissfully unaware of what was to come, sleeping peacefully between us.
'I love you David,' I said and grasped his hand tightly.
I watched, helpless, as the clock began its final ten-second countdown.
The alarm sounded.

I hate Monday mornings.

Julie Gray

ARE THEY?

Being alone for the first time in my life, this came about when Sarah started school, carrying a bunch of cherry blossom for the teacher, I spent some time sitting on the cellar window, staring down the avenue, I saw the back of a shining polished coach and mild sound of horses' hooves, I shook myself, could I be dreaming again?

Underneath the monkey puzzle tree, I found a bare twig with a hallow bore, good handle for a pipe with a chestnut conker already cleared out, all that's needed is an angled hole to affix handle, at four years old tea was near enough to use as tobacco. I slipped into the kitchen and found matches returning to the upper part of the pleasure grounds, to the cherry blossom to try out the perfect pipe.

Feeling dizzy and then I saw it, it was as though I was looking into a picture. The grounds were the same, very much more cultivated and a gardener was attending to the borders, another one was mowing the croquet lawn. Mammy's washing was no longer on the boxpalm, the horses' hooves was the first that I heard and then I saw the two jet black horses in full harness gleaming, drawing a magnificent highly polished coach like mahogany in the noonday sun. The coachman stopped the horses and a lovely little girl in a beautiful dress hair like gold, shimmering in the sunrays, her shoes were shining like mirrors. She came very close and smiled at me, saying
'Are you all alone today as I am always, I would like you to take a carriage ride with me, my grandmother, mother and my Governess Vickey.'
The adults of the group were in deep purple velvet skirts and jackets with lace frills about their necks, Vickey wore a plainer tailored dress with bonnet type cap with frill. Vickey was very kind, as were all the ladies, who spoke in a posh sounding voice, almost grand.

We took a route through the wood, round the garden walls, up another drive until we reached the greenhouses, ate some black grapes, nipped into the garden and picked the ripest figs. The little girl's name was Suzanne. She kept on talking about life in the big house, in its splendour.

All is gone now, it's a ruin I see and the grounds are gone wild again
and Sarah is pulling my arm saying
'How long have you been waiting for me.'
I am wondering will this happen again tomorrow, did I see this or was I
in a trance.

Later on at supper in the small house, my father and his friend were
talking about a little girl named Suzanne who died from Scarlet fever,
when she was seven years old, years and years ago. She loved cherry
blossom and used to sit under the one in the pleasure grounds, when it
was in full bloom and it's said some people have even seen her.
Sarah laughed 'They are joking?'
My reply 'Are they?'

Margaret Gleeson Spanos

DEAD ON TIME

That was all there was to it, or so he thought, standing with one hand on the bridge's stone wall.

Consulting his watch yet again, he sighed crossly. She was not coming. Strangely he chose the opposite direction to return. He glanced across just in time to witness her jump.

Juliet C Eaton

CHRISTMAS COUSINS

Late one Christmas day night, when the grown ups were playing cards,
cousins of all ages sat on the darkened stairs in the draughty hallway, all
huddled together. My eldest cousin said, in a hushed voice,
'Shall I tell you a ghost story?'
The younger ones said
'Yes yes,' whilst the little ones didn't dare speak.
'Weell' he said very slowly, 'it was a dark and stormy night,' he paused
and looked round at us all, 'and three robbers sat in a cave' another
pause, 'one robber said to another,' we all held our breath, 'tell us a
tale, well this is how it went.'
'It was a dark and stormy night, and three robbers sat . . .'
He got no further we all dived on him laughing with relief when we
realised it had just been a joke all the time.

Sheila Bates

RURAL GOINGS ON

A gossipy woman with fuzzy hair,
'All the village knows your cottage is haunted.'
'I've lived here for years - ' answered Mrs Camberley
' . . .and I've never seen a ghost, more tea?'
'Please - but I *feel* it . . .'
'Well, you may be right.'
Smiling, she handed back the cup,
Then disappeared up the chimney.

Joanna Carr

THE DINNER GUEST

She entered the restaurant on a cloud of floating white organza, bringing with her a sudden chilly draught. Her face was ashen and her deep, dark eyes stared at me as she came to sit at my table without asking permission.

'Good evening,' I said. She nodded in reply.

During the meal, I occasionally glanced over and found her staring back; thin, pallid lips pressed together in a weird sort of smile. A gold coronet was perched precariously on top of the woman's grey, wispy hair and I watched as her long, bony hands played with the spoon. This female certainly wasn't the dining companion I would have chosen. Even in this historic Castle Hotel, deep in the heart of Ireland's countryside, I doubt if I could have found a more bizarre character.

Throwing my napkin on the empty plate, I'd had enough of the silent treatment; I drained my wine glass and got up to leave.

'The meal was fine, thanks,' I said to the headwaiter as I paid my bill, 'but you might have warned me about the other guest. I assumed I would be dining alone.'

'You *were* dining alone, Sir,' the waiter insisted.

'*No I was not.* There was an old woman sitting opposite me. Did you not see her?'

I described her and the waiter turned pale.

'What's the matter, man? You look as though you've seen a ghost.'

'Not I, Sir *you* certainly have.'

Margaret S Browne

DAFFODILS IN SPRINGTIME

He unlocked the door, why rush in with a greeting. Melanie had told him on her mobile she was leaving him for David.

He heard voices but knew it was imagination. He left the door ajar, turning to look at the daffodils proudly lifting their heads, remembering when he and Mel planned how the garden would eventually look the following spring. The front door blew shut; he re-opened it, his head throbbing from so many tablets. He slowly mounted stairs to the bedroom, voices floated up.
'That door, I am sure I heard it shut again and yet no one is there!'
'Mel! Is that you?' He called expectantly, there was no reply, knowing how his imagination was in overdrive, he lay down and fell asleep.

Suddenly awake, people *were* speaking! Glasses clinking! He rushed downstairs to the living room it was full! Melanie walked straight past him, he followed her into the kitchen. She picked up her mobile.
'David, David?' she cancelled the call, 'What am I to do?' she anguished.
'What? What is the matter?' he shouted.
She ran up the stairs.
'Speak to me, damn you!' he demanded, rushing after her.
Putting on a hat, she glanced out of the window then left the room.
He quickly followed, the house now silent.
He ran into the drive, past rows of cars, yelling
'What is happening?'
As he reached the top car, his mother tearfully looked towards the front, the hearse was covered in daffodils, his favourite flowers.

Vivienne Doncaster

GAS HEATING: THE NEW ERA OF RUBBISH TIPS

'Image a city with no rubbish tips,
Funny thought really.
There were no dustbin men cos there were no rubbish,
Eye, when I were a lad, we 'ad open fireplace.
Could burn alt rubbish on fire,
not like now wiv' alt this central 'eating.'

Dawna-Mechelle

THE GHOSTS OF THE MUCH-REMEMBERED 'SHELBY HALL'

(Respectfully dedicated to both sides of the family)

Despite widespread public and private opposition, plans were well underway to build a hypermarket on some waste ground situated outside the town centre. The place happened to be the site of The Now-Long-Time-Demolished-Historical 'Shelby Hall'.

'Nothing can possibly go wrong now,' the foreman confidently spoke his mind.
'Everything is going very well,' his deputy formally advised him.
'All right,' the foreman continued, 'because we've all made such good progress on the site, we can finish work early.'
'The men will be pleased,' remarked his deputy.

So the workmen gathered their tools, and all went home.

That night the ground suddenly opened, as the deceased Lord and Lady Rumblestone left their graves. Then they started to smash all of the building equipment.
'No one is ever going to desecrate our graves. We will surely rest in peace,' they concurred.

'Whatever has happened here?' the foreman anxiously demanded to know, as he surveyed the true extent of the damage for himself,
'This equipment will cost thousands of pounds to replace.'
'We'll have to suspend all of our work until we have the repair bill,' commented his deputy in absolute disbelief, as he viewed the sight before him.
'So much for our first day working on the site of Shelby Hall,' sighed the foreman, 'somehow I don't think that the Rumblestones will take very kindly to our play.'

Michael Denholme Hortus Stalker

EATEN ALIVE

An alien parasite had invaded her body, she was being eaten alive.

Desperately trying to free herself, she struggled till exhaustion engulfed her body.

Awakening refreshed, determined to succeed. She dug her nails deep into her flesh . . . success.

The flea lay dead.

The cat curled up contented by the fire.

Irene Holroyd

SWEET TASTE OF REVENGE

The blade gleamed in the moonlight,
wickedly sharp. A woman had her limits,
she had reached her's. She was sick of him,
waking her up in the early hours,
arrogant, crowing about his conquests.
She gripped the knife, this time
she was going to have that rooster for Sunday lunch!

Susan Jump

THE VISITOR

Each winter night as bedtime drew nearer, I so longed for morning to arrive as quick as the dark night had appeared. I knew that when I was in my bed and the lights went out, yet again the visitor would appear in my room. I lay so still desperately trying to go to sleep so not to see this thing just standing each cold night by my door. I'd close my eyes tight but when I opened them again it was still there, just watching me, staring, not moving at all. What was this thing and what did it want? How I wish that I could sleep instead of just watching the thing staring at me. As the warmer nights came it did not arrive, but each cold night there it would be. I could hear my heart just pounding with fright longing for morning to arrive. With the warmer nights came the lighter nights and the visitor did not arrive. Then one cold night it appeared again but this time there was more light and there it was just standing, staring, watching me.

My old thick winter dressing gown hanging from my door.

Sue Belcher

2001

Farmers' foot and mouth hell
Sends cows to burning pyres
Nepal's Royal family gunned down
Liverpool football cup treble inspires
Estonia win Eurovision Song Contest
Independent for only ten years
Tony's toties rule for Britain
Four more years everyone cheers
But no orbiting space station
No Blue Danube future seen!

H Griffiths

AN ANSWER TO PRAYER

It was five years now since Greg had died. He had completed all the courses for ghosts, and had graduated with honours from the haunting school, he could rattle chains, make loud blood-curdling screams and he could move practically anything.

The problem was that he was lonely, Hector was quite good company, but he'd been dead for five hundred years and what did he know about clubbing, dancing or dating? What he really needed was a girlfriend, but where was he to find one? All the female ghosts he knew were at least two hundred years old, it would be like dating his granny. Each day he prayed for a girl friend.

Most of the newly dead entered the Great Light, Hector said that no one ever returned, so Greg decided against the unknown. Hector knew everything that was going on, he told Greg the Romans Ruins were being excavated and they needed experienced haunters to train the apprentices.

So Greg hopped on the bus, at least he didn't have to pay anymore, and made his way to the site.

'Line up,' he shouted, 'I'll interview you all in turn.' He started interviewing, weeding out the poorly motivated. The next person was a young girl, about his age, in shirt and jeans.

'Hello,' she said, 'I think I'd like to haunt but I haven't much experience.'

'Don't worry,' he replied with a grin, 'I'll teach you.'

Talk about an answer to a prayer.

Vivienne Cirelle

A WALK ON THE MOORS

hi neil,
    while walking the moors
one very dark night, something was to happen
to give me a fright.

i met up with a stranger so tall and so bold
and i'll never forget the story he told.

as i turned and asked shall we sit for a while
oh yes he replied for i've walked a long mile.

as i turned around he was no longer in sight.
oh yes that certainly did give me a fright.

then as I walked along a churchyard i did see
having gazed at one headstone i thought how strange it to be

then a voice from that grave no, not strange, it's just me
from the back of my neck
i could feel the hairs stand

as that voice whispered softly 'i once owned that land'
i read the headstone with my eyes filled with tears

for that friend had been dead for one hundred years
i still walk those moors along the same track
and often think of my friend and will he come back.

as i tell this story, it's not to boast
because he's not just a friend, he's also a ghost.

E Bradley

A PUMPKIN FOR HALLOWE'EN

'What's the matter Jane?'

'I'm so disappointed Mum forgot the pumpkin for Hallowe'en.'

'Don't worry,' said her friend John, 'we'll go to the pumpkin field.'

'But that's stealing and it's nearly dark.'

'I know a short cut through the churchyard.'

'No, it's too spooky!'

'We'll run, I've got a knife no one will see us.'

An owl hooted as they opened the lychgate, where they were joined by a friendly boy.

'Are you after a pumpkin too?' whispered John.

'Yes, I have come to help you, I know where the best ones grow, I've brought three candles from the church, my father's a rector.'

'Good, I've got matches and spoons for scooping.'

'Please hurry, I'm frightened,' gasped Jane, shivering under the yew trees.

'I'm not afraid of ghosts, the Rector's son assured her, I'll carve a lantern for you.'

Suddenly the moon freed herself from the cloud, flooding the field with ghostly light.

The boys selected three large pumpkins carving them carefully, Mike giving the first to Jane.

John struck a match, bringing the fearful faces to life, finding Mike had vanished.

Unbeknown, they had passed Mike's tombstone, twenty years ago, he had died, aged nine, from typhoid.

A E Doney

RETURN AT YOUR PERIL!

In Mesopotamian lands, in days of old,
Men worshipped gods who mined this Earth for gold,
Who from Nibiru/Marduk down here flew
Under whose guidance mighty kingdoms grew.
Should you return, bold Anunnaki crew,
We former slaves are now great 'gods' like you!

Alan Swift

THE NEW MAN

In one brief moment Simon knew.
The loneliness, the dread, the anxiety
of the past forty years was at an end.
Those who once scorned him for being a
devout bachelor now shook his hand.
'Congratulation.' Their words echoed
in his ears.
Simon had made the grade at last.

Michael Challis

WE SAW THE LEADER ONCE OR TWICE ATTIRED HEAD TO TAIL IN WHITE . . .

. . . Before the invasion army arrived wearing green uniforms. Wherever we looked they congregated in sixes or more, especially outside our residence.

Tried to get them to move on elsewhere to no avail, that seemed to incite more to gather. Shuffling around eating, until our green vegetables were devoured by caterpillars.

Hilary Jill Robson

FAIR PLAY?

His troubling shouts caught awake dorm mates with irritation. His eyes opened to browse the faces of worried peers who persistently asked 'Are you alright?' He replied in the affirmative yet it was the contrast with eyes closed.

The three previous nights were chilly with the same encounter with terror. He had been innocently haunted by a hunter who yielded an armoury or armament, but had hairy arms, bloody hair, a description fit for the brave.

He fought with slumber but had been defeated three consecutive times. Even in bright daylight, voices from afar bade him to sleep no more. Cynically, his envisions hated him. Yet, when bouts of tribulations and hankerings of horror visited at dawn, they all seemed to care.

His woe would stoop so low to pay him back. Unfortunately, the cost, the expenditure of trying times was too severe compared to the cause of murder. This tells the story:

In his childhood, naiveté started a fire that outed the dying candles of three neighbours. Everyone was ignorant of the truth except himself and his bosom friend, Brian, who passed away with the flames. Ever since, the cat had been hoarded in an airtight bag with no room for an escape.

That happened a decade ago, Now seventeen, a high school undergraduate, he lives to face the consequences of his action. He dwelled on a menu of grace, good and gaiety. Yet, close ones and even strangers seemed to reject him. Everyone kept him at arm's length, his loneliness was more than of a helpless baby in a lion's den. His solitude was not an allusioned form of fate, but beyond words: blood-curdling and spine-chilling.

Ato Ulzen-Appiah

VISITATION

She came to me - not elderly and confused - at noon, and she smiled at me, though my embraces refused, just as when she first met me!

I am light-heartedly enjoying the sunshine, for unexpectedly she came to me!

In the middle day I saw my loved one again - as she used to be! Young, with dancing eyes, no longer old and bemused, she came yesterday, just as in another life - - though she said she could not stay!

But she *did* come to me just past midday, made light my heart in me (gold sun was glad as me!), and left lifelong love with me!

As young as when we met, she came to me and smiled, then softly left again.

She came to me and smiled as of old. Now my heart sings!

Dan Pugh

A Mother's Plight

She was gazing out of the window,
as she did every day, when she
spotted the pyjama-clad toddler,
who had obviously run away.
As she snatched him up from the
screeching car, his mother screamed
from afar. From grief to relief,
to gratitude - quite a change of
                                                attitude!

Maureen Smith

THE VISITATION

My name is Ray, what I am about to tell you actually happened to me.

I am a widower of some years!

I met a widow Lyn and we decided to get married.

Everything is arranged, we are to be married in Church, the day before my birthday.

That night I woke feeling a weight on my feet at the end of the bed. By the moonlight shining through a gap in the curtain I could see a silhouette against the white bedroom door.

I know who it is!

I lay rigid in the bed, one moment hot, one moment cold. I dared not move.

After what seemed hours, the weight gently lifted off my feet and the silhouette simply disappeared through the closed door and I heard the words 'Be happy!' Wide awake now I lay still until the morning.

Lyn came round early that morning, 'You look white, as if you've seen a ghost.'

I said *'I think I have!'*

Ray Wilson

MICHAEL'S OPERATION

Michael has a second hip replaced
At Kettering General Hospital
While he is on the table
He sees three spirits
The first of brother Pete
Says he knows exactly why
In the nineties he allowed
Three girls to come to play
The second of his mummy
Knows he has a son
Paid below Britain's minimum wage
The third spectre he sees
Is of his mummy-in-law
She tells of his three kids in care
Because he said 'No' to toys.

They join hands and say 'Be gone'
And Michael does awake
As a baby in an incubator
In 3275AD as a girl
The lady in a green dress
Takes her home and names her 'Debbo'
Her mummy met a man nine months ago
Just for a quickie,
They have not seen each other since.

H G Griffiths

THE GHOST OF MARLOW

On a bright moonlit night in June 1941 a stray enemy aircraft dropped a bomb near the river in the sleepy market town of Cragton. It claimed the life of Jack Marlow who had seen his family safely into the shelter and stopped in the doorway to light a cigarette. He was killed instantly by the blast.

The large house escaped serious structural damage and stood a strong shelter for succeeding generations of Marlows.

But the ghost of Jack Marlow appeared down the years whenever danger threatened any of the household inside the great house.

The man lighting a cigarette waiting near the trees that had replaced the old shelter was the last thing Tessa Marlow wanted to see as she was on the brink of a new venture in the winter of 1950. Her private school for girls was bringing in fees to maintain the building and had lifted the threat of having to sell the family heirloom. A blackbird carved in jet with emerald eyes in a locked glass case in the art room.

Success gave confidence and dismissing the sighting of Marlow as a trick of the light, Tessa closed the curtains firmly on the evening shadows.

Storm raged outside as the school settled down for the night.

The next morning the sleepy market town awoke to tragedy at the new school.

The art teacher had disturbed a burglar who had forced open the glass case. She had given chase, and in her emotional state, run to her car with the jet blackbird clutched in her hand.

Knowing that the phone line was down in the storm, she had driven to the local police station and, going too fast, her car had landed in the river. Rescued from near death by drowning she had suffered a nervous breakdown.

The jet blackbird was returned to the school but the art teacher resigned.

'Was she the real thief scared away by Marlow?'

Freda Grieve

AN EMBARRASSED SCIENTIST

It was well after midnight and I walked alone as I always did. There was a full moon, maybe casting eerie lengthening shadows of bare gnarled winter trees, stumpy hollow ones, some ivy-girded to give them unusual shapes, all ideal hiding places for night creatures. So what? I'd seen it all before. Bats dived and swooped after night moths, feeding in the moonlight. Larger predators were also abroad: badgers, foxes, feral cats. These I hoped to see.

I wasn't superstitious. There was no fog, no mist, no wind, no dark threatening clouds. The marsh and quarry were surrounded with barbed wire and danger signs. All innocent, all normal, I thought. But not exactly. A faint inexplicable tingling shuddered my spine. The unease grew. The place seemed evilly chilling and mysteriously creepy. Why? I didn't believe in ghosts. Laughed at scary myths and legends. But . . .

My qualms became fear. Fright. Terror. These feelings overruled my scientific mind. That quarry *was* haunted! I stood petrified. Slowly rising out of the pool, a rag-veiled sinister phantom figure confronted me, with a raw scalp, bloody bones, and sharp pointed gnashing teeth. Getting louder . . . Nearer . . . Till the ghost grabbed me and sank those teeth in my neck. I lost consciousness.

They found me there next morning, still groggy. What beast had bitten my neck? Being forest gamekeeper, I was too embarrassed to tell. Would he ever haunt me again?

L D Allsopp

PAINT OR BLOOD?

It was a cold dark night and Angelica couldn't sleep. Climbing on her window sill she looked across the houses, there was nothing there so she stared at the stars. She had done this many, many times before. Her attention turned towards the garages that ran perpendicular to next door's garden. It suddenly seemed like daytime, even the trees behind the grey and blue buildings looked fresh and green. Then there were only the trees, as if she was seeing through the modern buildings. A new picture. Long grass, trees that bend and sway in the wind and a boy in old dingy rags playing catch.

Up, up, the ball goes towards the sky, then down into a tree. It's stuck, too high for him to reach so he begins to climb. Out onto the branch that holds his ball.
'No, don't' she cries. 'The branch is going to break; you'll fall.' She screams even louder. She wants to turn away but she can't. Snap! The branch breaks and the boy falls onto the spiked fence below. Then the picture fades and all is as it was.

Angelica walks over to the spot where the boy fell the next day. There behind the garages on the rails that separate the buildings from the graveyard she sees a splattering of red paint that runs down the grey metal. Still the paint remains, no matter how many times the rail is painted grey.

A M Williamson

THE KITE

The kite soared above.
The little creature kept low at the field's edge.
Little rabbits ran for cover.
The warm wind blew. The kite dived.
Grandpa wound in the line. Better go home now.
Your mum will wonder where you are.
It's well past teatime.

Clive Cornwall

WHATEVER BECAME OF JEANNIE?

It had followed her all the way down the road. Heart pounding, 'Puddum, puddum!' She carried on, petrified. The sweat trickling down her face. Trembling, she couldn't run, it was as though the thing had a rein on her.

She hurried on, with gritted teeth, eyes askew, murmuring, whimpering 'Go away! Go Away' through sweaty stinging lips.

Again she looked around, terrified. Oh my God! What is it?
She thought it looked like a shadow, but somehow different. Not quite the same, misshapen, pulsating, weaving and now lengthening, higher and higher, moving closer and closer. Jeez, it's stalking me, she thought.

'Oh God!' she screamed as the thing now came with a great rush, enveloping her. She couldn't move, in the blackness she saw lots of luminous haunted faces, all with mouths agape and hollowed-out eyes. Those faces were the last thing she ever saw.

Her body was never found, only a bag, shoes and clothes, melted beyond recognition, amid a pile of hard grey ash! A friend, had told police, that the last time she saw Jeannie, was when she had bid her goodbye outside their place of work. The Natural History Museum. And said; it was strange that day, as there was a blackness all around the building, and Jeannie was very quiet, and sad-looking, and told her friend that she felt something terrible, was going to happen to somebody, she was right, wasn't she?

Terry Ramanouski

OUR PARROT

He speaks the words of wisdom, and looks at you from the corners of his eyes. On his tongue there's definitely no lies. When he feels like it, he wants to fly. The sharp beak, as sharp as a razor, the signs of 'Don't judge a book by its cover'.

A Bhambra

EVERYTHING COMES TO THEM WHO WAIT

They queued all night on the pavement in the freezing cold. As dawn broke their anticipation grew. The next few hours crawled along on dragging footsteps until nine o'clock and the glass doors opened. Like a devouring wind the queue rushed into the store. The January Sale had begun!

Loré Föst

THE SHRIEKS

Time for a drink - then bed. As Piers filled a glass with whiskey given by a colleague, high shrieks began: *'Argh!*
                        A-argh!
                        A-aarrgghh!'

Windowpanes shattered - as did his whiskey glass. *'Why?'* he demanded of his family ghost.

As spilt whiskey dripped to the floor, it answered, *'Poison in your glass!'*

Chris Creedon

ONE MOURNING

Washing up after breakfast, I looked through the window; my parents, smiling, were standing in the garden, warmly clad for a winter walk in the countryside. Joyfully, I ran to the back door - flung it wide - they had gone, only the frosty garden remained. My parents died, several years ago . . .

Meryl Champion

SPEED TRAP

The car, tyres squealing, came into the camera's view, speeding way over the limit. Manoeuvring around the corner, he immediately swerved sharply avoiding the child. Hitting the wall instead, he flipped over, crashing to a grinding halt. Slumped over the wheel, encircled by flames, he heard the director shout 'Cut!'

Pam Wettstein

PORTRAIT OF A YOUNG BOY

A painting of a young boy was the only thing saved in the fire. The picture passed on to three more people. Each house burned down. After the fifth fire a fireman, knowing of the story, picked up the picture and threw it back into the house. The picture screamed!

June Clare

IMAGINE BRACKEN'S DILEMMA

Bracken rushed out into the garden, she
knew she had only a short time, checking
out the plants, borders and paths; she knew
it was there. Where, oh where could she have
left it? Mum called out, 'It's OK Bracken, I've
got it here, come for your food, tea's ready.

Carole A Cleverdon

THE GHOST OF THE DAIRY MAID

Stories of ghosts always fascinated me, an old dairy cattle man I once knew used to pass on many happenings he had or heard a long time ago. In a dairy farm in the Black Isle in Ross-shire in Scotland, there were many strange goings-on. About 4am on an early morning, you would hear the clattering of milk churns getting ready for the milk, but when you entered the dairy itself, the noise would stop, the belief was, something terrible happened to the dairymaid. He went in many times to find the byre freezing cold, with cattle turning their heads as if something was passing down the centre of the byre. He said the hairs on his arms would stand on end and the dog was the same. He opened the big byre doors to let the spirit through, although this wasn't necessary. He often tried to go in earlier to see as this always intrigued him. On one occasion he found milk churns moved to one side of the dairy, the place was knocked around as if the spirit wasn't happy, even the steam was turned on one morning; he often spoke of the happenings but no one cared to enlighten him, he felt the maid didn't like anybody interfering, but over the years it did get less, as if the spirit managed to find a friend in him.

Florrie MacGruer

GET A LIFE

She was seventeen, our Sarah, they never caught the hit-and-run driver who knocked her down. She died after two days on a life support machine. It was my fault, she died, my idea to separate in town, then meet up and go home together. But I was late that night and she'd left to walk home alone.

I saw her last night at Pete's party. Pete gave me one of those tablets, said they were brilliant, made you forget all your worries. I said I'd have it later. Then I saw Sarah. She was in the crowd, dancing just a short distance away. I couldn't quite see her face but it was definitely Sarah. I reached out to her but my arm seemed to float in the air as she drifted towards the exit. I followed her outside. Then I heard her voice from somewhere very near.

'Get a life Jayne,' she said softly, 'get rid of that tablet.'

I spun round and there she was. I tried to touch her but she bent away from me like a candle flame in a draught.
On a sudden impulse I spoke, hoping my voice might hold her.

'I'm sorry Sarah!' My throat was tight.

'It's OK Jayne,' she whispered. 'Just - get a life.'

Then she was gone. I went inside where my friend was looking at me. 'What's wrong Jayne?' she asked. 'You look as though you've seen a ghost!'

Anne de Menezes

MEN BEWARE
(Belt Versus Braces)

After sitting in the sun on a bench in the park, I tried to rise but could not, I leant forward and heard a click, and felt a sharp stab in the back, I jumped up, only to find that my braces had caught on the back of the bench.

Will A Tilyard

DID YOU EVER SEE A GHOST?

There was once a young woman who went to work for a shipping company. It was an old Indian family business, but they had decided, over the years, to take on staff who were 'outside' of the family.

The young woman had worked for the company for less than one week when alas! She was attacked by a gang of youths on her way home.

Slightly shaken, she returned to work the following day, and upset, she gave the owner's partner the news. They were also trouble for the owner's mother was ill in hospital.

The next day the young woman was called a stupid cow by another member of staff.

The young woman was upset at this but she continued to work. She knew that the Tibetans had been tortured and forced to eat grass before they were electrocuted by the Chinese because of their beliefs. She also knew that many Indians believed in a god named Visnu, a sacred cow, but she said nothing, although she was both perturbed and perplexed.

That night, the young woman heard the voice of a woman, although she couldn't see a soul about.

Frightened, she made her way into her flat and tried to relax.

Imagine how she felt the next day when she found the staff praying at the altar of the shrine in the workplace? Especially as the owner's mother had passed away the night before!

Colette Breeze

DANCING WITH DEATH

I awake late at night with the moon lighting up my room. Suddenly an overwhelming feeling of fear and coldness comes over me. I'm rising above my bed as the sound of old haunting organ music fills the room. Now upright in the middle of the room, I am face to face with a man in a suit. We're twirling around to the music (which is getting louder and spookier) from corner to corner of the room. But the man is a corpse, his lips stitched together, stitching down the left side of his face, his eyes wide open but face, blank and well dead. Yet an evil laugh from him entwines with the organ music. I smell the stench of death in the room. His laughter is chilling.

I look down to see myself asleep in the bed. Is this a nightmare or an out-of-body experience? Either way I want to wake up. I will myself to do so. I awake to daylight, the clock reads 11.30am (strange). There's a knock at the door. 'A parcel for Mr Fell' a man says.

'Sorry,' I reply, 'I've only lived here for two weeks. I've heard a Mr Fell lived here before me but I don't know his whereabouts.'

'Oh Mr Fell' says a passing stranger (a woman). Sadly he died last year.'
'Oh, I'm sorry to hear that the parcel man replies.'

Yes,' says the woman, he was our local church organ-player. The church isn't the same without him.'

Paul McIntyre

Don't Eat The Food, Just Run

Alice, Jane and Peter were playing in a large cellar, the cobwebs and the smell of must were everywhere. They had gone down a coal shute beneath a small manhole to enter the cellar.

Alice sat with Jane on a box, whilst Peter looked for treasure. They joined him, together they found a photo of a girl, large rusty key and a broken necklace.

Above the cellar steps the door opened, light footsteps of a man came down them. He put a large saucepan on a table. Leaving as quietly as he came, shutting the door quickly, then locking it.

Jane exclaimed, 'Let's get out now!'

Peter got hold of the saucepan, placed it on the floor and removed the lid. It was full of live red lobsters.

Shuddering he slammed the lid back on. He slid it away from him with his shoes.

Quite suddenly footsteps were heard from the cellar steps, but no sound of a door opening.

An old stout woman holding a plate walked near them, and called out, 'Chocolate cake, chocolate cake, you must be hungry Jenny, after playing so long down here.'

The petrified children crept towards the coal shute, struggled up, hitting the manhole open with a stone, got out. They ran dusty and dirty but unharmed.

Sarita Wooten

THE WHITE LADY

Lights out, all quiet in the hospital ward; curtains drawn along bedsides, with fronts left open. Lying there sleepless, I became aware of rustlings and whispers all around me; very eerie in that quiet ward.

Suddenly I became aware of a 'nurse', dressed all in white, standing by my bed.
'Funny,' I thought, 'all our nurses wear blue or green uniforms.'
She took hold of my left wrist, saying,' Come with me.'

My right hand gripped my drip-stand as I replied, 'No! I want to stay here!'
At that she tugged my left arm, so in panic I yelled, 'Help me, nurse!'

At that, the 'white lady' vanished as one of the usual nurses ran to me, soothingly saying, 'Hush, you've just had a nightmare.'

As she walked away I overheard her saying to another nurse, 'How peculiar; two weeks ago another patient in that same bed screamed. We found her clinging to her drip-stand, with her left hand stretched out, but she was already *dead.*'

Hazel Birch

MY LIVING END

Flowers swayed in the gentle breeze, their colours radiant and bright.
The sun shone from high above in the clear blue sky warming the room.
Through an open window I could hear the sound of birds singing, and
taste the clean air. A pleasant smell from the many mingling garden
fragrances lingered. My closest friends and family were gathering close
by. My eyes closed, I could sense their presence. Whispers about the
room gave clues that my life was ending. I knew this. I lay contented
knowing I had lived without compromise.

Not everything in the room was good. Something evil was present
which caused me to freeze in horror. My father on his deathbed had
spoke of something waiting for him to die, he was powerless to stop it.
This thing was watching over me, waiting like a predator stalking its
prey. Waiting for the exact moment when my life ended, to take my
soul. I could do nothing.

Its presence suddenly became stronger, the other people in the room
faded away. The dark figure rose up and moved towards me, it spoke.

'Come with me.' The voice was strangely familiar, it was my father's
voice.

'How do I know that you won't steal my soul,' I replied.

'Your soul belongs to me now, come with me, it is time.' As I looked
around I saw my empty body lying like a shell. People in the room
crying, comforting each other. This was my living end.

Pete Dean

GALATEA

Like a cicatrise of eclat cognisance I recall her at the soiree manifesting before my eyes in diaphanous splendour, cauterising the nurture of the moment, a mesmerising bellvadeor of translucent iridescence, a soporific caryatid of seraphic pulchritude, her mellifluous apparel of sericeous albedo etiolated in ensanguine sprusada upon her exiguous stature, her virescent eyes fulgent beneath her umbrose hair, pervasively elucidative to her demulcent physiognomy, saw eye spoke my sedentary trance and chanced a dance most enhanced by the music attenuating the impetus of our sagacious embroilment, whilst the band epitomised the threnody of our licentious philtre-ing through the irreguous irenic alcatoric alacrity of cadency when I noticed her aphotic lachrymose expression abnegating my proposal whispering the sapient illative of her soul

- Don't wish your time away.

She concurred before a condolatory fugacious flight into the irate deluge with chthonic sojourn. She was gone, vanishing into the crepusular occidence, leaving me imbrued and bemused in the doorway.

- What has happened to that young lady friend of yours whom you were dancing with?

Asking the inquiring host.

'I don't know, I replied still looking through the apparition in my mind,

- She just ran off into the rain.

- Rather peculiar that, I remember a girl quite similar looking do the very same thing at my last annual soiree, she continued phlegmatically lighting up,

- Found her drowned in the river . . .

Algid! I awoke where the seminal breeze blue through the curtains as it suddenly dawned.

Anthony John Ward

LETTING GO

She put his hand in hers.
The first day at school.
'It'll be OK Mum,' he said, and she knew he was right.
This was a big step - one they'd waited ages for.
Tears threatened as she waved goodbye,
went into the college and he drove off to work.

Sheila Smith

TIMBER

Once up on a time I woke up in a strange world
I turned around and saw a man say 'timber'.
It was too late. The tree fell. I died in my sleep.

Jake Shaw (9)

FIRST DATE

She simply had to buy that dress, this night was well planned.
Everything must be perfect. Once home, she ran the bath, it was to be
the works, face-pack, manicure - the lot. Heart racing - she slithered
into her stockings . . .

The doorbell rang - and there he was.

Wendy Watkin

APPEN IT WERE

The pall bearers lowered the coffin into the earth. The widow of the deceased threw a handful of soil onto it. Turning she said to her friend Ethel
'Well, that's ower, but I doant know who t'vicar were rabbiting on about. Twernt my Sam for sure. Appen it were someone else.'

David A Garside

20/20 VISION

It was bright against the night sky. It appeared to have a glow all around it. There were flashes of red and white as it crossed the sky. She felt frightened. She reached for her glasses and laughed. She could see it was nothing more than a plane.

Trudi James

PEAS IN A POD

A pleasant surprise when the vicar called
Chatting over cake and tea - 'twas
somehow heard an occasional plod.
Still we chatted - suddenly
something appeared to wiz past
puzzling us. Later mystified the
Vicar took his leave - but not
before we were bombarded with
'Sweet pea' pods bursting from their shells.

Josephine Foreman

LEAP OF FAITH
(Dedicated to my son, one of the painters)

The paint crews climbed upon the bridge they start from either ends.

Dangling like bright flies on old paper they glance at people by and by.

She walks alone the woman down below stands looking at the water how the river seems to flow then, with a leap she goes.

Jean Paisley

THE ANSWER TO A PRAYER

It had been an agonising trek over mountains, through forests.

They had not eaten for days, were parched with thirst.

Every step an effort, minds were giving up hope of reaching safety.

Suddenly lights shone ahead, a bright neon sign.

Their prayers had been answered, it was a McDonald's cafe.

Margaret Findlay

BACK STAIR

I was caught unaware,
As I was going up the back stair,
I met a man who was not there,
He appeared out of nowhere,
And fixed me with a glassy stare,
I did not speak, I did not dare,
At his wild, and scraggy hair,
Or old-fashioned felt hat and cloak,
He stopped me with a cold and bloodless palm,
Whilst my legs turned to ham,
At last the vision spoke,
Opaque and transparent,
To me it was apparent,
No earthly thing could be his parent,
he spake and was coherent,
In a voice, trembling,
Was he or was he not dissembling,
'In life I had no friends'
'Now I must return to make amends'
'Vain was I and greedy'
'Now 'tis my turn to be needy'
'I was like you, say a prayer for me'
'And speed me on to eternity'
So I said a prayer,
And wished him well,
On his voyage through hell,
All of a sudden he was not there,
I was all alone on the back stair,
He had vanished into air,
Vanished too through a solid oak wall,
Was left alone in that cold hall,

At that the dinner bell rang,
My heart sang,
Or I asking who or what it was, replied,
'Tis the soul of one who died'.

Alan Pow

THE GHOST TOWN

Tumbleweed rolls down front street.
Saloon bat wings swing, and bang in the desert wind.
The hitching rail is empty
Except for one tethered ghost horse,
And a shadow cowboy with his rifle called 'Lucretia Borgia'.
The spirits of Buffalo pound the ground.
Buffalo Bill is back in town . . .

Gordon Bannister

RECONCILIATION

She held on to life with all the willpower she could muster. The cancer had taken over her body, yet, gasping for breath, her spirit was strong. Drifting in and out of consciousness she heard a door slam, and then the sound of his voice . . . her son had come.

Pamela Gillies

THE VIKING

You came to Britain by longboat more than a thousand years ago, to conquer, rape and pillage.

Little did you know that after being garrotted by your own people you'd lie in clay, perfectly preserved. In a millennium be unearthed and displayed as a museum piece of Viking manhood.

Joyce Walker

THE NOISE

She'd looked everywhere, no stone left unturned. It came again, where was it? She would ask next door; opening the front door, there it was, a wee kitten, must have been out in the rain all day - she scooped up her mysterious 'noise' and took him in.

Iris Cone

THE BOY ON THE STAIRS

'There was a ghost boy! He sat on the stairs that led to the attic,' the old lady told me as she poked the fire. I see him on Saturday evenings as I go to bed.

She is not afraid, as he smiles as she passes she is alone so I visit her often, her husband has gone for his usual Saturday drink.. Looking into the dying embers of the old range, she says someone will die tonight, there is a hole in the cinders, she quickly pokes the fire, the hole has gone. She takes my empty tea cup, turns it upside down into the saucer.

'You are going to be rich,' she says, 'I see a lot of money here, looking into the dregs at the bottom of the cup.

'Tears are going to be shed,' she went on.

'I see a bird, a message will come your way soon.'

I laughed again, but she was serious.

'Tell me about the ghost boy,' I said, what did he wear. 'Old Victorian clothes,' she replied. 'Corduroy breeches, leather gaiters and boots. A red 'kerchief around his neck and a brown twill shirt and waistcoat of mole skin, he has a pleasant face, and he smiles as I pass him.'

She was in a sombre mood now and said, 'I shall sit in this corner and pass on (here in No. 3 Old Rectory).

I shall haunt this place for being turned into a museum!

It was time for me to go home, I thought a lot about what had passed between us.

There was a death, I had a message to say my brother had passed away in Australia, but I never became rich.

Lillian did pass away sitting in her corner, after eating her breakfast.

3 Old Rectory is now Cranbrook Museum, Kent. I often visualise her talking to the boy on the stairs.

Patricia Farmer

SIR PUDSEY

Hector grew up in a village called Pudsey. He was strong and handsome. One day a visitor asked him if he would like to become Lord Baggot's knight. Delighted Hector left the village, became a valiant knight, married Lord Baggot's daughter Petra and was given Pudsey for his loyal service.

Janet Vessey

A DARK WORLD

Discreetly observed this young child and mother seated before me.

Disturbing his hesitant, eager speech, vulnerable mouth, pallid perfection of skin. When after the journey she took his arm firmly to guide him safely, his wide-eyed gratitude revealed to me harshly his dark world of blindness.

Louise Rogers

POWER

The sea heard someone calling. This wasn't Poseidon or his Romanized son, Neptune. They'd had more respect. He was being commanded to stop. He bounded up the beach and watched the golden crown topple into his waves.

Who did this joker say he was - King Canute? King Knut more likely.

Pam Redmond

HIT OR MISS

The crowd was shouting and screaming my name. I could see them all, one side red, one side blue. And as I walked to the spot I could feel the pressure on my shoulders, like lead weights. I ran up to the ball and kicked it with all my might.

Kamran Ullah

TERMINATED

My heart started to pound faster. Nothing could stop it. I felt a shock of pain, as I scrambled to the floor and fell. I opened my mouth to scream as the figure approached me, but I was so afraid that I was incapable of speech. Suddenly my life terminated.

Saadia Jahan

Go!

I heard the blast of the gun in my ear and I jerked myself forward, feeling like a cheetah as it goes towards it prey. I started to run. With my heart pounding and my rapid breathing I crossed the finish line and collapsed with pain, holding the winner's medal.

Irfan Ullah

Out For A Duck

The sign said 'baby ducks for sale'. He had a pond so why not get some?

First build them a house to protect them in the winter.

He asked the shop keeper if they could sell him some wood. She said, 'Why do you want to keep plastic ducks warm?'

T A Napper

HEROES?

As they looked ahead, they wondered what it was that was driving them on, but deep down they knew. Then they fully realised what it was, it was the thought that they might capture the criminals and become heroes. It was a dream that had the possibility of coming true.

Helen E Schofield

NIGHTMARES

Eerie darkness emerges, suddenly I'm falling, falling, splashing violently beneath icy waves.

Struggling desperately, wanting freedom from black watery grave.

Gulping bubbles, float towards surface, fraying terrified limbs, searching for support, scanning towards surfing water waves, I'm drowning, my lungs filling with water, I'm spluttering, gasping . . .

Then I wake up.

Ann Hathaway

I WATCHED IT GOING DOWN

The giant aircraft wings were slightly wobbling,
as it closely flew right over my head.
It seemed to just miss a group of houses,
where people were asleep in their beds.
Slowly dropping down into darkness, and going out of sight,
it made a perfect landing using those runway lights.

Alan Brunwin

ILLUSION

It was twilight, as I made my way across the field near my home. Suddenly bright hazy lights like a ghostly fiend, hovered above me. Sheer terror enveloped me, as I backed away. Then I saw it, the eerie lights of the Combine Harvester making its way home for tea.

Sheena Pinnegar

TRUSTING HANDS

Rebekah held her mother's hand tightly, as they walked together, for her first day at school. After lunch, her teacher said, with outstretched hand, 'Come and play ball.'

At three o'clock her mum was waiting by the school gate, smiling, they ran to meet each other, with hands reaching out.

Ann Jones

ECHOES

She stood in the clubhouse kitchen, looking through the window at the pleasant scene - cup in hand as she finished the last of the washing up.

How many years had they been members? To far back, to contemplate! She smiled.

Bank holidays were always special days, when other clubs sent a bowls team to play in a friendly match.

The sun was shining so brilliantly today it was creating a misty haze, why she could hardly distinguish some of the players the heat haze making them shimmer, almost half transparent.

A loud burst of music made her frown, years ago the fields next door were home to seasonal fairground activity. The hula-hoop stalls and merry-go-rounds, the children's delight, can we go across to the fair Mum.

Mum can we, tugging her apron strings in childish anticipation. 'Yes,' she said giving them a handful of coppers, it was a long day for them at the bowls club, and in those far off days quite safe to let them go just a field away. She frowned, since the fair had long moved on several discos had made their annual meetings there, unofficially of course. The click of woods and a blast of applause bought her back to the present. The match, half over the players making their way in for tea . . .

Joyce made her way into the building, she usually got there early to set the disco up, making sure the lights and loud speakers where working properly. She looked out over the garden, the council had kept that part when they sold off the old bowls club. What a to-do there had been about that, cries of, 'It's tradition, all the years of hard work, keeping the greens in top condition.'

All the young players coming up, who would there be to groom for the England team, if small clubs like these disappeared, still it's 'progress' as they say, and in this the new century, even royal wishes were ignored. Why a few months back the golf club that the old queen had given part of Hampton Court Gardens for 'use of my ordinary subjects to use as a golf club' had been leased off to a wealthy American club. The desolate faces, looking out from the TV screen, all the money we poured into the club, taking the youngsters with us, so they could get interested, no compensation, and we won't be able to afford the new club fees, she sighed, 'Progress?' 'Well,' she frowned, 'yes as usual on these bank holidays, on these quiet moments before she switched the music on, she was sure, she could hear the click of woods and applause from an unseen crowd. She shook herself, and switched the music on, 'echoes of the past' you'll be saying they can hear you next. She smiled at her fanciful thought, why each would think they could hear ghosts next.

The bell rang the crowd arrived, and life went on.

Gladys Mary Gayler

OUR RUN

Couldn't keep up with Sandra. She had been a keep fit fanatic for years. Each day I improved though and we both ran the 'Fit for life' charity run. She came in second, while I was trailing near to last. But I made it. I felt great.

Jeanette Gaffney

EMILY'S ROOM

Bunking off school was a regular thing for Peter and Sean, a couple of tearaways who cared for nobody but themselves . . . but they were soon to change their ways.

At nine o'clock precisely, the two fifteen year olds headed for Blackhill manor . . . a derelict old house long since abandoned. Within minutes they had forced entry, lit their first cigarette, and opened a can of lager. Then Peter produced a couple of tablets. They are known as crack, and can have disastrous effects when mixed with alcohol.

Sean heard a noise from upstairs: 'What's that? . . . someone's up there,' he said in his drunken stupor.

Both boys staggered upstairs to the end room, passing furniture covered with dust sheets and cobwebs. They opened the creaking door, and saw a girl playing with her doll. She was about ten . . . 'Hello,' she said, 'my name's Emily, do you live here? My Mummy and Daddy are the cooks for the master, we moved here in 1785.'

The two boys were stunned, then Peter said, 'You mean *nineteen* eighty five don't you?' Back downstairs the boys concocted a plan to get rid of this little brat who may shop them. They planned to throw her down the well outside.

Slowly they crept along the hallway, and opened the door . . . their eyes widened. The room hadn't been disturbed for years . . . dust sheets covered the chair that Emily had sat on, and the cobwebs lay thick everywhere.

Peter and Sean stopped playing truant, stopped taking drugs and drink, and eventually became model pupils . . . all as a result of visiting Emily's room.

John Topham

BREAK OUT

They heard the patrol warden pass,
'Now,' said Helena, jumping from the window.
Martha followed, nervously.
With trees for cover, they soon reached the bus stop.
But their luck was out, they had to return.
'Been trying bingo again,' said the warden, opening the door of the
protected housing.

Kathleen Mary Scatchard